Speaking English
Poems for John Lucas

Edited by
Andy Croft

Five Leaves Publications
www.fiveleaves.co.uk

Speaking English
Poems for John Lucas

Edited by Andy Croft
Published in 2007 by Five Leaves,
PO Box 8786, Nottingham NG1 9AW
www.fiveleaves.co.uk
info@fiveleaves.co.uk

ISBN: 978 1 905512 12 6

Five Leaves acknowledges financial support
from Arts Council England

Five Leaves is a member of Inpress Books,
representing independent publishers
www.inpressbooks.co.uk

Cover illustration: Pauline Lucas
Typesetting and design: Four Sheets Design and Print
Printed in Great Britain

Contents

Speaking English

Speaking English brings together over a hundred poets from four continents. The occasion is the seventieth birthday of John Lucas, energetic teacher, prolific poet, critic, reviewer, literary historian, publisher and editor.

Assembling these poems has not been difficult. Everyone whom I invited to contribute to the book has done so. No-one wanted to miss the opportunity of paying tribute to John. He has himself contributed generously to a number of *festschrifts* for other poets, several of whom here return the favour. *Speaking English* includes writers of regional, national and international distinction, old hands as well as emerging talents. Unexpected guests mingle with the usual suspects. They represent several distinct but overlapping cultural worlds — small presses and little magazines; adult education and universities in Britain, Greece and Australia; the New Left and Old Labour; cricket and jazz.

Thirty years ago, John was my second-year tutor at the University of Nottingham, a formidable if sometimes forbidding figure who seemed even then to have read everything; who was always inspirational. Among so much earnest dilettantism, his insistence on the seriousness of literature and on the seriousness of its social obligations represented a revolutionary challenge to our thinking about books. Later John invited me to Loughborough to give my first poetry-reading, and published one of my first poems in *Critical Survey*. He took issue with my first book of criticism in *Socialist History*, published my second book of poems at Shoestring and published my edition of Randall Swingler's *Selected Poems* at Trent. Recently, as editor, he included two of my poems in Five Leaves' *Poetry: the Nottingham Collection* and offered the manuscript of his *Flute Music* for my small press, Smokestack, to publish.

Everyone in this book will have similar stories to tell about John's encouragement and generosity, usually announced in his unmistakable but barely legible handwriting. But there are probably three enduring reasons why so many writers have wished to celebrate John's birthday — his criticism, his poetry, and his role as an editor and publisher.

John's published critical works are many, from all those single-author studies — books about Dickens, Crabbe, Lawrence, Clare, Goldsmith, Bennett, Gurney, Gaskell and Blake — to the wide-ranging arguments of *Tradition and Tolerance in Nineteenth Century Fiction; The Literature of Change*; *The 1930s: A Challenge to Orthodoxy*; *Modern English Poetry: from Hardy to Hughes*; *England and Englishness: Poetry and Nationhood 1700-1900*; *Writing and Radicalism*; *The Radical Twenties;* and *Starting to Explain*. This is a remarkable body of writing, by any standards, comparable in scale and significance only to the work of Edward Thompson and Raymond Williams. It represents the quiet development of John's own version of an English Marxist literary criticism, engaged, scholarly, close readings; studies of the regional, the urban, the plebeian, the radical and the real. His criticism has always stood up for "the ragged-arsed" against the forces of political, intellectual and imaginative enclosure, against what he has called "Bloody England.//Bloody class. The common bloody shame."

John has published eight books of verse, from *About Nottingham* (1971) to *Flute Music* (2006). His translation of *Egils Saga* is an Everyman Modern Classic. I can think of no other contemporary poet who has so consistently made such extraordinary poetry out of ordinary experience and everyday speech. His is a democratic art, located in the provincial and the plain, but constructed with learning, craft and wit.

Almost all the writers in this book have, at some stage, been commissioned, edited or published by John — at the Byron Press, Faber, Merlin, Trent Editions, Five Leaves,

Greenwich Exchange and in magazines like *Renaissance and Modern Studies,* the *New Statesman* and *Critical Survey.* Almost half have been published by John at Shoestring. Most will have read at readings he has organised in Beeston, the suburb just outside Nottingham where he lives. Several contributors were once involved in editing *Poetry Programme,* the University of Nottingham student magazine which he helped to start in the 1960s. Many will have read at Loughborough or Nottingham Trent Universities where he has also taught, and organised readings.

Speaking English is not a book *about* John (although he has a walk-on role in several of these poems). Instead it seeks to address some of the subjects which have engaged so much of his attention over the years — England, literature, cricket, criticism, history, teaching, publishing, politics, poetry, beer, jazz... And like the best of John's own poetry, these poems celebrate common experience, the regional and the radical, the demotic and the democratic, the poetics of saying what you mean and the politics of meaning what you say.

Some are old poems. A few have been published elsewhere (a few in the special issue of *Critical Survey* celebrating John's sixtieth birthday). But most have been written especially for this book. Many were originally dedicated to John. I have removed these specific dedications because it should be clear that all these poems and the whole of this book is dedicated to him with admiration, love and affection.

Andy Croft
Middlesbrough
February 2007

Observations of a Mortal

Katerina Anghelaki-Rooke

"Our love will be of a higher order"
said the gossamer one as he was leaving
and his gaze was rolling down
my lips that were dripping poems.
I don't know what he meant; the truth is
there are many things I don't understand of late...
That character bending there, for example,
  with every possible detail
explaining how he wants his dinner.
This woman here, buttoning her dress
with so much concentration, as if
her whole life depended on it.
Such precision in demands
only a guaranteed eternity
could justify.
Oh! Look at that fat woman
she can hardly move
and her companion is even worse, he is
  dragging himself...
And yet, this finished female
won't have a single grain of sand
on her spotless foot.
Her male must dance in the air
provided he rinses her sandal to perfection.
But here she comes, the lady, she approaches me
  quite by chance,
dressed by now. Of course she doesn't know
I've been describing her.

Same with God, I thought; if he existed
we would never know if we were creations
  of his imagination
or if he is describing us and having fun.

Interruptions from the Past

with apologies to Octavio Paz

Alan Baker

My grandfather would sip his pint,
and talk of Keir Hardie,
George Lansbury,
a voice for the working poor.
And the tablecloth shook like a banner.

My father would stir his mug of tea,
and talk of Atlee and Bevan,
Beveridge,
the birth of a Welfare State.
And the tablecloth shook like a banner.

I kept quiet:
who was there for me to speak of?

Someone Had To

Samuel Plimsoll MP, "the seaman's friend", campaigned
fiercely for safe loading limits for ships

Michael Bartholomew-Biggs

Being on the ship that didn't sink —
the one in five survivor — made him
somebody who had to cry
enough of coffin ships that wallowed
out to sea with overloads of risk,
police-escorted to deep water —
no escape for crews across
the side that law and order took.

He manned his campaign platforms with their widows.
Veiled and silent walls of sadness
loomed behind him, night by night
relentlessly, like long black waves
to add momentum to his rhetoric
for overcoming one by one
the flagships of the owners' lines
of unseaworthy arguments.

How often there is something going on
it's clear someone should try to stop:
how seldom someone does — and gets
small thanks until they're good and dead.

His Bill was twice thrown overboard. He salvaged
just one watered-down, bedraggled
clause on painting loading levels —
at the company's discretion.
Freeboard being fixed might harm free trade
so anywhere would do below
the deckrail or the funnel: coasters
could still ride as low as barges.

Before the marks were set by seas and seasons
he'd worked himself almost to death.
But near-drowned men do not forget:
mourners stripped off Sunday best
then let the sweating, black-plumed horses go
and took their place to pull his hearse
like galley slaves who'd volunteered
for this one coffin's homeward run.

When someone's good and dead, the things they changed
are how things are: the way things were
is what they took on board till they'd
submerged themselves way past the safety line.

A Cautionary Tale

Nick Beddow

John Lucas!
I wrote you a long essay
once
And you returned it longer
Every margin crammed with your red ink
I showed it to my mother
Look at that
At least he's read it
More like fucking bled on it
said my father
who swore
and I copied him
B minus it declared at the top

I've tried being minus
but you hauled me up
Every comment sound
and sage
So bless you guvnor
A tip of the hat and
Three loud squawks from Sidney Bechet

I shouldn't have copied your beard,
mind

Postcard from Bruges

David Belbin

We're on a short break in an ornate town.
Day trippers have quit the chocolate box scene.
Three hours were enough for me, too. How come
everything here's so old, yet so clean?

Only the dank, drain smell from the canal
curdles the sweet ambience. A bird calls.
The hotel painter shifts his ladder with care,
continues to whitewash white, spotless walls.

I found the above in an old notebook.
Its last verse worried about influence:
how to avoid what's been said before,
stay mysterious, and hide my ignorance.

You'd have told me, small things matter. Tone.
The way a sentence flows, length of line, while
what's borrowed, copied, stolen, means far less
than if you've got or you haven't got style.

Two English Sonnets

Peter Bennet

St George's Day
For centuries the same sun has been sinking
here where we loiter to invoke
the green, embroidered by long-fingered shadows
of branches coming into leaf, the drumming
and piping over, and the people —
who danced today and work the land in common —
cupping hands into the cool mill-brook
which are our own hands, but with callouses.
Beside the inn door, at a solid table,
a ballad-seller and two dairy-women
sing the language we are thinking.
As Hob the landlord gobs for luck
into their ale, and picks his nose,
new worlds grow outward from the sunlit oak.

Black Country Browning
Here's where the forges were, the crucible,
where we fought fire and smoke and sin
to cast a fancy from a flower-bell
or catch a sunset-touch in glass
for chapel windows that began to glow
as far as the antipodes.
We coupled on the warm stone by the furnace,
which brings us down to thee, grown up so well
without our piety or taste in verse.
We burnished hammers with our skin,
but it consoles us that our bishops knew
of chorus-endings from Euripides
as we sink deeper where the anvils rust
into the centre of the compass-rose.

Guardians

Remembering a writer and an artist he admires, and honouring
them and, too, his own inclusiveness

Paul Binding

Christmas Eve, and the burning logs
she believed in, and that long-ago event
she didn't, and beyond the windows
the bare West Dorset hills, dark
guardians now of darker wild garden
(through which a stream tumbled like music)
in this long slow hour before
the crimson curtains were drawn.
Lining all walls of this rectory room
books, old books (what undying arcana!),
and in the corner the engraver at work,
who'd apprenticed himself young to Bewick
and brought back all his patience with trees,
birds, leaves, rabbits, dogs, the magic of
wood and stone against our *mal-de-siècle*.

She stared into the fire, spectacled eyes
in her lined triangular face, and softly said:
"She'd have loved a dog. She always wanted
a dog. I should have let her have one!"
But the woman she spoke of had died
a matter of days before, and so
her/their dog lived only in wood-smoke.

I was beside that fire too, thinking
of someone else dead at Christmas-time,
four years before. She had wanted to lie
in Dorset too, forever in sight of
the Purbeck bays she loved: my mother,
buried instead in that commuter-land
she'd neither liked nor understood.

8

This Christmas trio — I now think
the hills outside were quietening us
into the true conversation that runs below
all meetings of living beings but is too
rarely heard. My companions were
devout servants of peace; I believe that evening
I learned from them. And yet
odd things now plague me from that distant hearth:
how she who'd tramped hills as a cat-adoring
witch, and visited all ranks in the English past,
had dropped no tears for battered Hungary
in her zeal for new world order; how
the engraver shuddered at every incursion
of commerce as if to save England from itself;
how I, for whom suburbs spelled loss,
refused to make them any repayment,
and how my mother, that stranger there,
had nattered on at me to do my best
in their gloating opinion. Well, perhaps
we never achieve consistency. But I hope
the hills I'm living among now remind me
that tramping feet and steadying hands
and peering eyes are often so much wiser
than what we let into our needy heads.

Perennial

Nadine Brummer

Had I been able, I'd have bred
a rose for your seventieth birthday
to be called by your name,
prolific as our *Ferdinand Pichard* bush
that peaked this year. Flowers came,
six at a time on a single stem,
mottled pink and white, disclosing
in each of them a variousness
of width and depth in bars and lines —
magical the way magenta works
its design. What colours accrue

to a *John Lucas* rose? A red,
ardent enough, perhaps, combined
with blue pitched like a saxophone
playing a Miles Davis number,
or that Blue in Green improvised
by sun on the sea in Greece
where no two ripples are alike.
No, had I been able I'd have bred
a lucid flower that grows as if
a swirl of light had settled down
to deepen its glow.

Listen to the Stories

Jim Burns

So, imagine the scene,
a bar frequented by musicians,
somewhere in New York,
and in walks Charlie Parker.
He goes to the jukebox,
inserts a couple of coins,
and then heads for a drink
as the music starts to play.
Country and Western: sad songs
of lost dreams, broken hopes,
midnight trains, and even
a happy time or two.

When the music stops,
Parker goes again to the jukebox,
and again chooses to play
some Country and Western sounds.
After the third selection
a well-known jazz bass player
turns to him, and asks,
Hell, Bird, what is it
with all this corny stuff?
and Parker looks at him,
and says, with a little smile,
Listen to the stories, man.

From Manual

Richard Burns

The young wives toil uphill ferrying water
and by the well the old ones knit and sew
They are reeling in the ships far out at sea
darning and mending aftermaths of wrecks
snipping and bordering frayed hems of lives

Even the strengths and directions of winds
and patterns of eruptions on ocean floors
get stitched by their gnarled fingers
and what they do they do
scarcely noticing the effects they achieve

***

Outside the café underneath the plane tree
the old sailors play backgammon
Little they know or care about pasts or futures
who once chugged out past overhanging islands
and caught shoalfuls of fish in their long nets

Islands reached stony fingers out to grab them
Hidden rocks and reefs sharpened their nails
Waves grew claws to slash at them and snatch them
Darkness itself unleashed invisible talons
and now they sit outside the café like ordinary men

***

By the well the *tricoteuses*
can afford to chat and pause
Their hands are in no hurry
Once they had dancers' feet
Now they are all fingers

As they chatter about this and that
delicately intent but
seemingly without effort
their hands carry on regardless
like busy spiders

This Is Not the Poem

Derrick Buttress

The poem I had in mind
would have been precisely engineered,
one of those intricate structures
with softly reverberating chambers
and inescapable rhymes,
a work praised for its inevitability,
like a cathedral, or a solo by Chet Baker.

The poem I wanted to write would be
a piece of mechanical perfection,
like one of those telescopes that scan
the furthest reaches of the night
and move on a single bearing, silently,
turning to encompass all that's known.

But no... This poem turns out
to be just another ramble with the dog,
both of us sniffing in the undergrowth
for something new to say
in lines as slack as a slow day in Filey.

Just another show-off,
like a streaker at Trent Bridge
tossing aside its intimate garments
as it runs — its lilywhite stanzas
and it chiming rhymes,
abandoning its artful prosody
until it is naked and free —
free to be what it was always born to be.

Aqueous/Vitreous:
the Humours of the Eye

Catherine Byron

Mine eye is glassy.
My mind glazes over.

> The globe of the Earth
> is enrobed in a gel of air,

Can I see in a glass darkly?
What text is being glossed?

> In water, light can bend
> even an iron bar.

You must enter
a *cloude of unknowynge*
to glimpse your god

> put on shades
> when you do your slow pavane
> before the gloryhole's

white heat.

There is a hiddenness
in so much of the making.
Even the hot-glass artist
must walk away from
bench and gloryhole
and offer up the piece
to a waiting kiln:

Just-blown glass
tapped free of its iron
and placed in a hot kiln
to cool down slowly

    annealing unseen
    overnight.

Just-poured glass
still reddish with heat
trailing gloryhole glory

    annealing unseen
    over days.

Glass for cold-firing
stacked in the mould
or in a reservoir
poised above it

the drain-hole waiting
to swallow down
the glass as it softens
gathers and pools

to run at last
into the mould
evenly, fully,
and then to anneal —

    its metamorphoses
    its soaks and relaxes
    all, all unseen.

Miner's Lamp

Adrian Caesar

How to go on with this labour in the dark
while sun blazes from towering skies
and barbecues ignite in suburbs with no worries?
At the beach surf's up, the bikini tops are off
It's all good, mate, is the new mantra
as we shrivel under the glare and slip slop slap
the sunscreen to stop the cancers;
greed is the fuel, consumption the fire
Shop in the name of love the brassy slogan
for an Aussie Valentine; poetry's dead mate
forget all that crap the post-doc, hip-hop
priest of pop announces to bright young things
media studies are the go: no need to verbalise
the visual image is where it's at — you can view the
bodies clearly or what's left of them, no worries:
analysis is easier when you can see the lies.

And I think of my great-grandfather and his sons,
their lifetimes down the pit, Mosley Common no. 3,
interrupted only for a bash in France and Flanders
the Somme, Paschendaele, they did their bit
undecorated, then back to hacking out a face,
on their knees, swinging pick and shovel in the black,
the sulphurous dust clogged throats and lungs,
their skin scabbed and scarred and seamed by coal,
which fuelled the nation and the empire
but never lined their pockets; they lived
for pride and washed it down with bitter pints,
Eee, that's grand lad, didn't touch the sides,
as nothing touched the hardness of their lives
the strikes and the disasters, carrying out their
mates who'd died, they coughed themselves to sleep,
and at the last stood arm-in-arm, shouting United.

I hear them when I find the going tough
when I lose belief and curse my bitter gifts,
imagining myself in some twilight space,
which is just another avenue for decadence.
Tha's never done a day's work in tha'life,
I hear the colliers say, narrowing off-shift eyes
against the dazzle. By way of small reply
all I can do is try to mine their legacy,
knowing it's easier to chisel out a line
than do eight hours hard labour,
I'll take the cage down deep as I can go,
try to hew the richest workings,
remembering they had scant reward and no applause;
the wealth and warmth and light they gave went
unremarked and at the end left nothing but
black and rugged nuggets, their truthful shining.

I.M. Peter May, d. 28.12.94

Angus Calder

You play therefore you are: I write therefore I am.
Writing is play: your playing makes me write.
We are the moments we have been together,
days out of time, creating our own weather,

and out of time, or in that real time,
not pettifogging minutes, but the true
time which stands still, as if forever,
May walks out to the wicket, shy and clever.

Oval my paradise: a sheening green,
May in his perfect whites, his long sleeves buttoned —
that cover drive will flow, I know it will.
It whacks the boundary board, I hear it still.

As fast as Azharuddin's or Kanhai's
most wristy shots, most perfect executions,
May's drive, the body leaning with no violence,
speeds over Paradise: one hand claps: silence.

Our different kinds of play are all we are
worth having — moments when the timing works,
as when May's forehead rises with his eyes:
six over deep mid on, time beyond lies.

Siegfried goes down the Rhine towards the crash
of middle-Europe in mid-century.
Wight, a neat black man, catches Peter May,
the cover drive an inch above the grass.

Oh willow, willow — Tricky Sam is wailing
above a distant delta, plunger mute...
Strange fruit: May tried to play ball with apartheid.
I find no rhyme in that, nor reason either.

Rhyme falters, the clock ticks and Egypt dies.
Lungs wheeze, legs fail, all facts are ash and error.
You play the simplest exercise — my heart
(a metaphor) is flushed with timeless art.

The contradictions can't be reconciled
within clock time. That art resolves one issue
is never proved. Forgiving Peter May
I can say this, though — you must play and play

"for tenor, horn and strings", for other horns,
for Miles, for Brain, for Hodges and for Grace
and Ranjitsinhji, batsmen now the air
we breathe: you must play, because you care.

Natural and classical or modern, let
that ripeness ooze as only you can make it.
Most elegiac of all instruments
the horn subsumes our lost, and found, contents.

Piano

After hearing Einaudi

Philip Callow

It goes on,
the snowdrops gathered in full force,
the birds in a steady procession
to their table,
the daffodils all tight, waiting their turn,
the bus to Evesham
finding the library
where it has always been.
It goes on
like the flood of piano notes,
beating and then hushed
with their different rhythms,
as if nothing has happened,
nothing at all.
It had been like this before
and now is so again.
It goes on and so does he,
rejoicing as he hears the piano,
effortlessly accomplished
and inevitable
like the drawing of breath.

The Great Things

Gerry Cambridge

The difference here is space:
Your sight gets used to searching horizons:
That speck is a merchant tanker.
Is that dot of a person tourist or local?

Here there is hardly shelter:
To step round the gable at dusk is to be hit
  by a gust from Iceland;
The house sails like a ship through a squall
That is gone in a swirl of bouncing water miles
  off in minutes
Rattling the panes of crofts on the further islands
Smudge-blurred under that big black;
There's a single brilliant field.

In this green flatness
Crofts are small grey insurrections
In the dictatorship of Atlantic weather;
The one pink cottage is a made-up girl
In a scatter of old thrawn women —
The dwelling for the summer warden of birds
That the international visitors come to see: the shrieking
City of terns on the North Hill,
Scraps of feather as white as the island's church,
Its stone incandescent in stormlight under the
  blackbright cloud.

No child has been born here for fifteen years:
On the west shore
The silent congregation's whiskery, patched with orange,
An arrested stagger of drunks on the backdrop
Of cobalt white-flecked sea in Atlantic wince-light
  of the gusty days.

This evening as I walk down the road to the phone
There are spreading gleams on the pewtery plain
Of the sea to the east as if some great beast might
  emerge there
Pouring like waterfalls, and with a roar;
Down on that shore
Tommy Mackay's TV is on, from the smudge of light
  through his pane;
The remote fantasia of *Coronation Street*.
On the left as I pass, a meadow-spread back,
Netta Groat waves from the kitchen window where she
  washes the plates;
Five miles east she can see as I can, tiny down at the
  foot of space
And striped like a barber's pole or a mint,
Drawing the eye right down to it,
North Ronaldsay's lighthouse, late-sunlit —
Visibility that means rain.
And, in an hour,
While the islands' windows wink to rectangles of butter,
The silent sun will descend into the distant
Stadium din of the west:
A brief exhalation of rose, from over the edge of space.
The wisp-pink clouds will fade to a gustchill grey.

Elsewhere the great things of the world will be
  taking place.

Borders

Peter Carpenter

Ground Floor between *Fiction* and *Poetry*.
The second time in as many days. It comes at me.
The smell from where she sits between *Travel*
and *Crime* is enough make browsers wrinkle
features in "what is <u>that</u>?" disgust. She stinks.

Because clothes for sleeping rough, layer upon
layer, are being walked in, underneath the visible
leather-sheen great-coat and cap. Auschwitz?
That liberation shot at the wire? No, here, beneath
the *3 For 2 CD* offers in the Borders Summer Sale.

The truth is, she impregnates every last page of verse:
the entire Carcanet list, the brand new Armitage,
the Collected Muldoon, the Selected O'Hara, the new
Billy Childish, *101 Poems That Will Change Your Life* —
you name it. We all track on by, join a queue

to pay by plastic. She exits into Market Square, freeing
up from under the cap her long streak-grey hair,
making her way beyond us. I keep finding
her days later, unremitting, unbearable still, in page
after page of Paul Celan or Miklós Radnóti.

The Sunday Academicals

Malcolm Carson

Henry Winterman's I think they were
that sketched the tactics in the air

at least the strategy we should have used
before our best hopes were abused.

But still with clever reinforcements steeled
we'd scatter fitter hopes across the field

with Parfitt's mane and shining studs
launched at those much younger bloods.

Rodway's critical approach,
eschewing fallacies to poach

some practice on tutorial walls,
would just produce a lot of balls.

And Johnson, Eastwood's, Ruskin's glorious son,
would leap and catch the ball for fun

while Carson, goalie, beret in mud,
would remonstrate, spitting blood,

stamp on the hat, questioning the need
for someone with his feline speed.

McClelland laid aside his pipe,
his study of The Mob, to swipe

those who presumed to greater prize
by dint of skill, or perhaps of size.

Lucas commanding our splendid field
rose high above to restrict the yield

of goals we always gave away
before belatedly we'd enter the fray.

Dickens, Clare, Bennett, Gurney
you felt he'd mustered for the tourney,

Louis Armstrong, Colyer, Randall
(Boycott's run-out was a scandal).

Then to Beeston's Oak to embroider tales
of heroic deeds with Shipstone's Ales.

Water Work

Carole Coates

This was the best that Henrietta Scott
could manage. She hauled water from
the pump in Drury Lane up five flights
to her room in the waterless house. She clanked buckets
to scrub Covent Garden floors — straw, shit, mud,
gobbets of phlegm, cabbage leaves, egg, the bloodstains
  of beetroot —
all excised, scoured and sent in filthy water
through gullies, drains and gutters
and gothic passages of sewers down
to the ponderous important river. She swilled out privies;
carted water uphill, upstairs; scrubbed attics;
washed out cellars when the sewers flooded.

She was my great great grandmother.
Her daughters became washerwomen.
These women who carried water from pumps and wells
had raw chapped fists, backache, throbbing chilblains,
prolapses, arthritic knees, varicose veins, T.B.
Their bodies are intimately connected with mine.

                              Let water remember.
Let it leap from the tap crying "your mother did this
and your grandmothers". Water, remember them all.
Henrietta Scott. Water, remember her
and Sara, her daughter, and her sister Rose.
Remember them all hauling water when water was rigid,
holding tight in winter, when gritty drippings
hardened to ice and windows thickened and bulged with it.

Let water remember them.

Iridium Club, New York

Mandy Coe

Mined from darkness
fired and beaten, golden
flower raised to cold kiss,

a finger-run of noteless
practice. Take aim – push
breath up
from red-black to light,

sliding notes off arching stone
to herald the pomp of kings, or stir
the low hip-sway
of body-heat.

Air and air and air.

Whale-blow of spit,
warm gold in purple velvet.
Latches shut.
The waiter
collects empty glasses.
The drummer pairs his sticks.

To a Cornet Player, Prematurely Retired

Barry Cole

So, no more Sister Kate
Perdido Street
or Limehouse Blues

no again Downhearted
Swing Parade or
Gatemouth, Darktown

won't play Somebody Stole
My Gal (Weeping
Willow Blues) or

Ory's Creole Trombone
will not return to
Tight Like That

and what of Empty Bed
Blues? After You've
Gone? Got No Blues?

But you'll still hear, hidden
in your waking dreams
those Farewell Blues.

Red Ellen

Andy Croft

"Middlesbrough is a book of illustrations to Karl Marx"
ELLEN WILKINSON, 1924

She stares out from the pages of *New Dawn*
As though the future needs to be out-faced,
Her flaming red-flag tresses to her waist
Among the endless fields of unripe corn.
They christened her Red Ellen, Little Nell,
Miss Perky, Fiery Atom, Little Minx,
As if to say this cold, old world still thinks
All fiery reds are burning brands from hell.

In Jarrow and in Middlesbrough today
The flames of change are embers in the grate,
Cold fires of ash and dust that illustrate
How much we all prefer the colour grey,
Still too distracted by the colour red
To see the fire that's waiting to be fed.

Dorchester Pastoral

Simon Curtis

Bridleway and beech-trees,
With robin-song and rook,
And sloes and old man's beard
In hedgerows, too — but look:

Below the wooden footbridge,
Front bumper in the stream,
A burnt-out joyride Peugeot
Mucks up both mood and theme;

In Indian summer sun,
Faint skeins of cirrus high,
The hatchback dumped and torched —
For heaven's sake, just why?

Schadenfreude impulse?
Binge drinking dare? Or joke?
Excess testosterone?
Amphetamines or coke?

Twenty thousand quidsworth
Of high spec tech gone west;
So much for Barnes's Dorset,
And all the rural rest.

The Ballad of the North Wind[1]

George Dandovlakis

Master North sent a message to all boats:
"Boats out at sea and all passing galleys,
cast anchor in harbour; for I'm going to blow hard,
cover vales and mountain peaks with snow,
and freeze all springs and fountains. And take note,
whichever boats I come across in the open sea,
I'll have them wrecked upon rocky land!"
No sooner had the boats heard his threat
than all made for harbour, except one!
Captain Andreas' galley still sails in the open.
"You do not scare me, Master North, however hard
  you blow!
My boat's made of walnut wood, and my oars of beech.
Its keel is of bronze and its mast of steel.
The sails are made of silk, fine silk from Prussa,
and its ropes from a fair lady's hair.
I've chosen the crew with care, each one a fine warrior
and a young sailor who can forecast the weather;
and whenever I set the boat's course,
nothing can make me change it!"

"Now, up the mid mast, my boy!
Check the wind and choose the time to sail."
The young sailor climbed up with laughter,
but now comes down in tears.
"What did you see up there, my boy?"
"I saw the dim sky and bleeding stars;
I saw the thunderstorm break and flash;
the moon grew pitch black; hailstones and lightnings
fell upon Attaleia's ridges."

[1]*This ballad is actually a dirge sung in commemoration of
sailors lost at sea.*

No sooner had the sailor finished
than a huge thunderstorm broke out
and the boat's rudder began to creak.
The sea foams and rages; the masts shake and splinter;
Waves rise high; the boat shivers and quakes.
A blast of wind strikes her one side,
and a second blast strikes the other;
A third blast hits both sides
and breaks the hull to pieces;
masts and sails cover the sea
and pallikars fill the waves.
Now the young sailor's body
drifts forty miles away!

All mothers weep and console each other,
But there's nothing to console a young boy's mother!
She gathers some pebbles and stones, fills her apron
and runs down the coast. There, she stands
and throws her stones at the sea
scattering the pebbles on the waves:
"O sea, bitter sea, sea with bitter waves,
You've drowned my son, my only child!"
"It's not my fault, poor me,
nor are the waves to blame!
It's the ship-builder's fault, who made his boat
too weak to withstand the wind's rage!
So, I'm losing my boats, my ornaments, so dear;
I'm losing my brave sailors, my fine singers!"

Like Nothing Else in the Habitable Globe[1]

On reading the letters and journals of Dora Carrington

Kathryn Daszkiewicz

Virginia loved the way her purple words
tore like a mayfly up and down the page.
  She wrote just like she talked, her friends observed,
all in one runaway rush. When her ink was green
  the lines would dance. Minute was minuet.
She couldn't spell — once told of a *sogjourn*
  (which might have done if it had poured with rain)
and felt annoyed — I can't make it look better.
  Her quick nib spiralled out mistakes she saw
but most remained. Small letters mixed with
  random capitals
  spawning eccentric words to twin with thought.

[1]*The quotation which forms the title of this poem is Virginia Woolf's description of Carrington's letters.*

Dr Johnson

Barbara Daniels

He's lumbered with huge flesh and heavy bones,
bent nearly double, twitching, gulping food.
In other men a flame-like mind disowns
the body's weight and its inquietude.
His reason cannot tell him how to live,
how his light soul could fly above disease:
this monstrous carapace will never give
the spirit time to separate with ease.
He knows the two are different but his frame
is so convulsed with crippling, black-dog fears
that in half-madness they become the same.
The wolf gnaws until selfhood disappears.
 And as his mother dies, he sits and writes:
 he'll pay her passage with his darkest nights.

(Johnson's mother made him read *The Whole Duty of Man*
every Sunday. "On hearing she was dying, he did not speed to
her bedside but plunged into writing 'Rasselas', exculpating
himself by earmarking the proceeds for her funeral." Roy
Porter *Flesh in the Age of Reason.)*

Perama

Tassos Denegris

There's the mountain
We came upon
Suddenly there before us
On the high school

Excursion.
Treeless rocks
Same emotion
End of the earth.

A landscape
Of horror, and you know
It's been haunted
By the corpses

The swelling up
Of the Asians
From the naval battle
Of Salamis.

Coketown, England

Alan Dent

It's evening and the traffic's growing thick
in Coketown where the smoke once made us sick,
all smokeless now,
the post-war zones imposed
to clean up lucre's muck;
and to the suburbs people flee
not seeking scenes where man has never trod,
but, with any luck,
to catch their favourite programme on the telly
where they can see
some wannabe exposing too much belly,
and flop down on the sofa knackered, spent,
in front of what's got common over time,
to see pride raised above simplicity
which is supposed to make us all relent
from strife,
as if we've made our peace with god
through electricity
and need no longer try
to make ourselves at home
between the grass below and the vaulted sky.
And Nat Gonella once blew fine notes here
and Kier Hardie raised some hope with words
but all that's gone,
we're modern, though I fear
Gradgrind's reign in schools is not quite done
and Bounderby's still castigating workers
for wanting turtle soup and silver spoons,
the shirkers!
Stephen Blackburn might still feel at home
and shake his head at lack of providence;
at last we've got a petty right to roam

though on his every fence
the Duke of Westminster writes bold
KEEP OUT or PRIVATE.
So we live on postage-stamp estates
while aritos get subsidies for theirs.
Who would have guessed these old
relations, past their sell-by dates,
could keep us in mad thrall
to robes and furs?
Oh, would that Robin were amongst us still
and from that town set up by Saxon Snot
could shower justice arrows for us all
so no more rich or poor, high or low
we'd drink as equals in the Trip or Bell.
The polis though, I think, is ill,
the *demos* fears its *krasis*,
the Paycock struts and Joxer hears
the world is in a terrible state of chasis.
And yet, let's raise three cheers
for what we've got
and say: To hell
with time-servers and tossers!
Three score years and ten,
Owzat!
A life of poems, books and comrades
notes from Bechet's horn and Tatum's fingertips.
Take up your pen,
we need you still to bat
and thrash these slick young blades
around the park.
It's dark,
but Coketown's light with promise yet
the mean old lock-out men have had their chips,
a new world's being born you've helped to make
and have you more to give?
Oh yes, you bet!

At the Poseidon

Alan Dixon

Looking for trouble
to make something to say
for the long hot day,
sand bodies and sea
and brown breast wobble,
he strode to the middle
— in a pause in the music
and clinking of glasses —
of the crowded taverna,
where no foreign female
had failed with the boys,
and shouted, "Greek men
are the best in the world!"
The cheering was loud;
they raised their glasses
(so fond of the English)
observed by a frowning
Byzantine nereid
and brought him a bottle,
and brought him two,
and said it was true.

Summer Ash, East Lane

Sue Dymoke

Last to show its hand after winter,
Ash shivers grey-green fingers
high above allotments hidden behind
corrugated lock-ups, boarded half gates
and former front doors renumbered
neighboured now by hawthorn and privet.

Rivalled only by fully clothed holly,
Ash dominates the wide lane where
backlit meadow grasses catch last
light and berries race towards ripeness.

A flagship tree, its wide open mast,
putty bark towers above pear and cherry,
quince and bramley, superior to hasty colonisers
dense, undistinguished sycamores,
waiting for autumn helicopter glory.

The watchman looks on over crumbling
bothies and wounded greenhouses,
patched up plots and lost orchards. Ash hears
hedgerow rumour of thefts and deaths,
concealed weapons and border skirmishes.
Ash listens to toads stir and shift in dry undergrowth
plop of frogs returning to source,
stutter and fizz of hoses over
dry dust, reluctant scarlet runners.
Ash absorbs the flap squawk of greedy pigeons,
the magpie squabble and shrill to
and fro of robins as each pair scours
new turned soil for brood food.

Ash oversees the wide lane where
bats circle and swoop towards the light
to snatch their evening meal in gathering dusk.

To the west the sun sinks pink and slow
beyond a blackening tracery of apple boughs.
Foxes lazy from too much late afternoon sun
leave flattened spaces
(always the same flattened spaces)
and sinew their way through hedge gaps
(always the same hedge gaps)
before loping off down the lane.
Their eyes prick alert
to dodge headlights on the Mansfield Road.
Tails twitch ready for the nightly duels
where they will mewl like strangled children.

Ash accompanies a blackbird's evening call,
always sung from the highest branch,
with its own timeless shivering.

Somewhere Like England

Robert Etty

Cracking snail shells on plant pots, a tiptoeing
thrush taps out morning's fresh poetry,
catching the ear of the white cat that yawns
as it curls on a car's warming bonnet.
Ten birds sing ten new songs from chimneys
and hedges — or is it only ventriloquist
starlings mimicking dawn for dreamers
in pale dreams of somewhere like England?
A man's wandering past with a labrador,
dog eyeing a cat that hasn't stopped yawning
and man eyeing the lane's dark-on-light camouflage
of shadows and wetness a shower sprinkled
there half an hour ago when (before sunshine
broke out) raindrops were pinballing down
through the ash leaves and teasing
wet ticker-tape out of the willows.
Where cow-parsley meets itself changing
direction, he turns for the country side
of town, whipcracks the lead so his labrador
follows, and pauses there, looking at things
that aren't happening — unless it's the call
of a cuckoo that halts him, a cuckoo
calling in somewhere like England, that

silence until it cuckoos again.

Little Jazz

Roy Fisher

Trumpet-players, all too often
beset by narcissism, heroism
leadership, hypochondria
the flourish, the pain of it all,
call for our understanding
and deserve it.

But the plucky one had to be
Eldridge. Even when no sound came out
you could still tell what he meant.

When the Buddhas of Bamiyan Fell

Kate Foley

for one heart-shocking moment
before the censor kicked in
it was satisfying as the slow collapse

of a factory chimney — or earth falling off
her axis, as you know she will.
Our lips flickered,

a little replica of that great bald fragment
of smile that lies in the valley dust.
Why did they fire their rifles,

shout with glee at wounded trickles
of rock while a watching child
clapped his hands? I remember my mother

once lay, a sleeping giant in the moonlight,
her inscrutable limbs sculpted in silver.
Had I known DEAD

I would have sent it's hot golden bullet
straight from my cot to her heart. Not gods
anymore, the Buddahs of Bamiyan,

made part of our own flesh by the long fuse of hate.
Now in our sorrow, none the less true
for being late,

we must carefully bend to our task, piece
together all the shattered Mummy's and Daddy's,
the Humpty Dumpty's, foolish or wise,

finding a kind autumnal patience,
which after that first small greedy lick of pleasure,
may come to us if we wait.

A Word with Ralph Fox

Mike Freeman

Back in our Halifax, *compañero mio*,
Grime's power-blasted off the town-hall walls,
Its gilded tower touched up, new civic piazzas
Opening on tapas-bars, but you'd still recognise
The old wool merchants' Piece Hall though
Their mills have gone the way of handloom weavers.

You'd not so easily recognise, Comrade,
Your Party, pressure-blasted off the streets,
Unwoven piece by piece, its mills demolished,
Though CP-chic boutiques still retail
Retro-modes, recycled mantras, make-over
Shades of red turned greenish greys.

But ever the Quick Brown *Zorro* you had heard
The baying pack of history closing in.
I have to think you'd seen that even then
In Spain the rot was spreading, the Comintern
Destroying most of what you thought it fought
For. But *have to? Most of?*

Some's there in your ten years' argument
Against myopic engineers of culture, your
Polemics against agit-packaging — though isn't
Your *Life of Lenin* hagiography? How long
Would you have thought the Good Old Cause
  stayed good,
The Party was the only game in town,

The hand that history dealt you? Fascists
Simplified the issues till Lopera
Guaranteed a final solidarity
Of ashes in an international grave
By some *arroyo* among olive trees,
Sparse cover against bullets, none from shells,

Along the road that Lorca's rider took
Knowing he'd never get to Cordoba,
Promised city. By the time you died
All promises were being ripped up by Moscow's
Systems and psychopath. Now, *compañero*,
The company's declared bankrupt, auditors

Are picking among the bloodsoaked archives.
New blood congeals in cold, hot, proxy wars
Fuelled by oil, American imperium,
God-propelled certainties, the globalised market
Marx predicted — but he's marked down, author
Of just another narrative to pick and mix.

Remember Lister Lane, Ben Rushton's grave?
Last weekend we were clearing round his headstone,
Brushing up Marx and Blake as well to shine
His Halifax Chartist epitaph. And yours?
After this note (for the talk we never had)
Instead of inscription, here's a postscript:

On a car-park bench you've got your local plaque,
The balance that the town's account admits.
The council thought you'd taken the wrong track
But history wrapped as heritage acquits.
You'd claimed our Chartists back for centre-scene,
Cleaning up their old bricks to build tomorrow.
(It's not just agitprop will shake the screen:
The Ritz is showing *The Return of Zorro*.)
The Fascists are back in Halifax, no arm-bands
But a shot-silk warp for every old-style weft,
So you don't need telling what your town demands:
A Popular Front (you know the rhyme), broad Left.
So welcome back, though Leninism baulks.
Zorro@socialism.westyorks

Young Lester

Roger Garfitt

He rolls the only dice
      at which he never loses
so quick and light the sixes
      fall beyond belief

The New Orleans Strutter
      the kid who had to Charleston
to his own horn has the room
      at his fingertips
all eyes on the freaks of touch
      that are conjuring notes
from the by-ways of the metal
      bluegrass leaps
back country blues
      and C-melodies
transposed for the tenor
      as if the paces
of the unicorn
      were to be found
in the horse

      All the accessories
are still to come
      the hieroglyphics
on his cuff-links
      the matching suede shoes
with every suit

but already he has
his call — that little hoot
          as he goes up in the air —
and his calling
          the light tones the hipsters
will take into their cabbala
          and sing under their breath
as alive as the dust
          under the shaded lamps
of the pool room
          to the ascension
of the everyday

Epitaphion

translated by *Manos Georginis*

Stranger, by the Ganges I repose,
a Samian. On this thrice-barbarous soil
I led a life of pain, suffering, and toil.
This tomb, with the river close,

encloses tribulations a-plenty. Pure greed
for gold goaded me to gross trade.
In a storm on an Indian shore I was laid
then sold, a slave. Until old age, indeed,

I toiled, laboured without laughter,
yearning for a voice from Greece and the distant
shores of Samos. Hence, I suffer no evil this instant,

nor do I fare in mourning in puissant
Hades. There with fellow-citizens I shall be resident.
And speak in Greek hereafter.

C.P. Cavafy (1893)

High Summer 2006

Duncan Glen

It is this sunny day in Fife, so names drift out of
memories still moving in the far away.
                           Slab Square
a meeting of ways, a Nottingham that I walk
through by street signs, named buildings. First
by Chaucer, Shakespeare, Dryden, Goldsmith, and
Byron. But what of Philip James Bailey
working on his *Festus* for fifty years? Can he be
leaning still on that bright sign by the Arboretum?
I guess not. Set in stone he does look down
from the restored Castle. There fires
once burned in the riot of 1831. Is that Henry
Pelham Fiennes Pelham Clinton, fourth
Duke of Newcastle, still trying to turn the
Reform tide from Clumber Park?
                          I can visualise
Scott, out of Edinburgh, leaning on a sign
by the Arboretum that says Waverley building.
Does that passing art student recognise
Sir Walter? I think not. Poets can be dated.
There is 15th July 1824. Did
thousands truly see Byron lie in state
in the Blackamoor's Head in Pelham Street?
There is 1812 and we know that
Ned Ludd had a bare cupboard and an empty belly.
The sun is hot for any procession to
Hucknall Church.
               But
a first, a spinning mill, Arkwright come to
town. Is the Mill pub not renamed in Hockley?
You tell me, John, the Nag's Head is now the
Lincolnshire Poacher. The Bell Inn must

survive, students are eternally there. That, John,
we surely know. I saw hammers strike blows
into the rock of the Hand and Heart, a new space
created on Derby Road. The alternatives of being
70 years of age hold forward. The caves
of the Trip to Jerusalem need no hammered
extensions.
                Does the name Zebedee
Jessop still live on under John Lewis
in a Milton Street that moves beyond month
or year? Yes, *Paradise Lost* can be dated
as being printed and for sale from August
1667. Yes, in 1879 George Gordon Byron was
living with Mr Gill at no. 76 St James Street.
Yes, John, your Byron Press can be given a
bibliographical start and an end but
the elegant lines of G.S. Fraser
out of Leicester's Stoneygate cannot be
confined. You tell me George and Paddy's
daughter is now MD of the Penguin
Group. Also, yes in Beeston, a shoestring
has been given an extending meaning.
                            Now it is 1994
and John Clare, wearing no hat to be
doffed, has professors confer in Nottingham
Trent. And we know his memory is not
lost. A naming between the lines, his face
reflecting in the river with the sky.
                        It was once only. But
who can forget 1985 the year Freuchie
villagers out of sunny Fife went to Lords
where nostalgia masters memories. So you said
of Trent Bridge, John, where names recur
and grow fabulous!
                    And now,
memorably, OK surreally!, Lord Byron,
George Gordon, out of Aiberdeen, drifts down
the Trent with D.H., out of a recurring

wood, and Frieda von Richthofen, as was,
out of an unconscionable hour — or two!
They meet, surely, at Trent Bridge with
Randall, centurion hero of the lost
centenary match Down Under. It was
Melbourne and March 1977. Days of such
sweet madness when by the Trent the sun
surely has got his hat on. Derek is saying
nothing to Lawrence or to Frieda or to
Byron, or anyone, but together they are
seeing swallows flying free out of nowhere
for many a *sun drenched Saturday. . .*

Delivering Learning

John Gohorry

Who can free Buccho
imprisoned by walls of silk,
ignorance, longing?

What should Buccho learn?
Empty mind. Who should teach him?
Buccho must teach him.

You talk, and outside
the classroom rain teaches you
what it is to speak.

From the place you are
you appear as a stranger
in the place you were.

The lesson ended,
and afterwards Buccho learned
it had not ended.

By Way of Invitation

Andrew Graham-Yooll

Always thought that Nottingham
is not that far from Hurlingham,
not really.
Six thousand miles or so, that's all.
Tourist Class
could crush the best travelled kidneys,
perhaps that's why he never ventured
South.
Here they'd like to see John Lucas
for the cricket.
He is, after all, a man of travels.
Cricket has been played in the Plate
since the first British military landing
in 1806.
It failed.
You read about that in the Army Museum.
The visitors were repulsed by the natives,
English merchants kept up the cricket
with calls in a form of Spanish, now.
Good poets here, too, great jazz
fusion with tango, samba, chamamé,
politics.
Each summer of ours,
his winter,
we think he would like the cricket,
jazz, fusion, tango... politics.

(Note: Hurlingham Club is in Buenos Aires.)

Reading John Clare on New Year's Eve

John Greening

If we'd had his Fen eyes, we'd have observed
the mouldiwarp still tunnelling the paved
enclosures: mareblobs, witchens, pinks and pooties
beyond our striplit broadcasts. If we had noted
his words under our engine's hum, the names
that aren't from dead-leaf catalogues of dreams
but rooted in a real place, we'd not be fooled
by furred Celebrity, but know Fame's cold
bleak teeth and face its keeper when he's hanging
his catches on our Auld Lang Syne, singing
of what cannot be changed, not what's on sale.
When we had heard that distant New Year bell,
we would be carrying his black truths by heart
across our thresholds, not thumbing a remote.

In Praise of John Clare

Barbara Hardy

Clare
loves

the minute
grass blade bent wet
minnows crowding a spring's soft-water dribble
pad of mud or moss and the black-snail

the individual
random idling wood path
flavour of south-west airs
rifted oak reeling or battered gate that claps
sweet hay he knows is withered grass
snipe lying low in the flags and many nests
the pettichap's
hay and dry oak lined with down
its eggs scarcely bigger than peas
smooth of silk grass and yielding reed
snow feathering trees

and the green
poor persecuted weed
scrambling frantic
yes childhood's puzzle
dandelion they said pee-the-bed don't pick
of course stinging nettle
but daisy or bluebell
hard to tell
flower or weed.

Clare
pours
over plant and creature
peers
in face
and feature
looks at the looking back
may at times declare
himself in faded flowers of speech
but black
in madhouse and weeded enclosure
recalling unparcelled now purloined space
will mispell faithful and clear
his dead fresh love in a world's hurt and lack.

Radio Fun

John Hartley Williams

Warm cabinet of sound
be known again to me.
Let *Cushion Foot Stomp* forever haunt
the stag-faced lobby
of Godalming Hotel.
O radio tune thyself
to voices Britisher than mine —
clarity-bones and banana-tones
not to mention zeal.
Talk me through the mystery.
Give me Music While I Snooze.
Let me hear the spaceman's words
go wonky as the dullness
of a sermon from St Ethelreda's
monsters him completely.
Let John Arlott
tamper with the seam.
Let chaos be delivered to the pitch
as umpires shrug
and raise a finger at the moon.
Have Billie sing the blues,
my father grab the off switch,
while I defend
her melancholy-jocund squawk
till death.
I want the weather to be dismal.
Let half of Cornwall disappear,
and London, under fog so thick,
you hardly hear
that Hilversum
is reaching out in Dutch to rescue us.
Hilversum. O Hilversum.

Bright prairie of foreign names,
let me ride your range.
Let your voices draw closer
to the chair of my ear
where I crouch
above
my white attention.
Let me rise through listening,
a phoenix out of boredom's ashes,
to hear *The Washboard Five*
shoot the antlers off
The Monarch of the Glen.
Have everybody
duck.
Wireless, be my guarantee
that there is
something I can like round here.
Let that waitress slide
with me together
down the moaning curves
of Buster Bailey's clarinet
to roam the illustrated dial, the world
that whispers far away.
O let me press
the baffle of your speaker fabric
to my far gone ear. Have
ocean breakers
and a mew of seagulls waft
me to a tryst upon a raft
with someone else who likes
a toady tune
like me....

Middle and Leg, Alfred, Please...

Peter Hay

"...this bloke's leering face, and then, one delivery later,
his forehead printed redly with a new ball's seam — he's
worth remembering...."
ANTHONY LAWRENCE, *Cricket*

And so I take poetic guard,
fat, fifty, heaving an asthmatic's wheeze
up the pitch at the Demon Lawrence —
hunter of heads,
fell mangler of the batting flower of a backwoods
  generation.
Pinger betwixt eyes.

That's now.
Then it was thus:
fat, forty, heaving an asthmatic's wheeze
up the pitch at a faceless, infinitely exchangeable,
smartarsed, supercoiled, mononeuroned
Flash-Harry-cum-Spring-Heel-Jack
all fit to burst with flex and strap and swagger;
the bristle, the cock, the couth, the *savoir faire*
of a low-grade psychopath.
So come on you smalltown bullyboy,
you strong-in-the-back, weak-in-the-head,
subtle-as-a-brick-shithouse
artless young berserker.
Come on — take the old bastard out,
drop it half-pitch and fly for the eyes...

And see the old bastard deep in the crease
slip inside,
see the bat's nemetic arc,
the light fleck at the penman's soft wrists...
and that dull thwack is no man's head,
but a small dark sun vanishing against the cypress line,
a sweet, doom-drenched spot of red
climbing, climbing to the mid-wicket fence...

Once it was thus.
But today I read a poem:
Cricket, by Anthony Lawrence;
and now those faceless, interchangeable,
mad-galloping, flinging, cursing, sulking
overbrawned quicks
have attained their face and fame,
a single personhood
to wear through all my smug and dreaming days.

Anthony, it is you.

Nocturnall

Stuart Henson

Hardly the year's midnight, but the blank hour
that you wake in and just can't sleep again,
  too early to be called a dawn.
  February; bitter; the car
   small on the roads, a toy.
Unfrozen for an afternoon, the sky
has smiled a tight-lipped smile and turned away —
that kind of emptiness. The world's a husk.
Odd street lights flicker, crystal in the dusk.

To drive across the map of scarp and dip —
Rockingham, Uppingham, the sweeping spread
  of the Vale of Belvoir sprinkled
  with week-old snow — is still to slip
   back through a melt of words:
these boroughs and these burgesses, these woods
clinging like balding remnants, and the roads
asking their way to parishes. All this
a cipher for what England is — or was.

Returning, as you spin between the walls
of drifts, the shining signs are all you have
  to prove the car has not sheered off
  into black space, a dud capsule
   propelled at the future.
You're glad to see another human creature
reel home from a shuttered pub: his stagger
proves that the earth turns as it always did,
warmed by the whisky-laughter in his blood.

The spread estates of Corby are alive,
but only just, at 2 a.m. A town's
   decline: an index of the times.
   Things struggle on; you can survive.
    What made the front page once
is old hat now: it's more than four years since
the rocket-gantries of the furnaces
came down. The fences moved on up the road —
the lamps, security, the all-night glow.

For journey's end, a slow countdown of names,
worn and familiar: the signposts blink
   Lowick, Titchmarsh, Bythorn, Brington,
   Molesworth, Catworth, Tilbrook... home
    in the brittle frost-dark.
And you pity the fox in the white arc-light,
the police at the gates, their talk like smoke.
Tomorrow's headlines (but too late to hold)
YOUNG MOTHER AND TWO CHILDREN DIE OF COLD

Legacy

Gordon Hodgeon

To the young men — who all on earth are blowing it
in cars, on bikes, in minibuses, tanks and helicopters
et cetera, you young exploding over one hot planet
care of wheels and tracks, under wings or rotors,
blowing your thoughts and beliefs out, your fertile seeds,
prayer books and hymn sheets and political posters
that lift and drop their feathers of fireweed,
the dust into the dust into the dust —

I leave: my delight in autumn sweeping this churchyard;
a weather-wormed cross, sandstone, sharp by it
bright flowers all grief; words that double the doubt;
each child of mine and each child's child;
words that breathe and outdance me in the warmed air;
the blood's habit surging my heart there and there.

Bibliotech

From Riddle 26, *The Exeter Book*

Graham Holderness

He had it in for me, that certain someone
Who ripped off and stripped
The flesh from my skin,
Dunked me and dipped me,
Dragged me drowning, sopped
And sodden, sluiced and soaking,
Wet from the wash; stretched me out tightly,
Painfully pulled, pegged unprotected
In a searing sun, for days and days of
Dry desiccation, dehydrating
Drought. Then slit and sliced by the
Hard-honed gravel-ground keen knife's
Edge, fiddling fingers furled me in
Folds. A high-flying fowl's finest feather
Sucked up ink, scratched on my surface
A glittering stream of wood-dark dye.
Beyond the brown brim the plume
Plunged, dank and dripping,
Scratching and stabbing, scoring my
Sutures, tracing its track.
Was he the same one, my erstwhile enemy,
Who sought me and saved me from
Torture and torment, bound me about
With a bulwark of boards, tightly textured
From well-tanned hide, graced me with gold,
Twisted, tensile, brightest beauty of
Blacksmith's work? Was he indeed
My friend after all, that inscrutable stranger
Who turned me from textile to tell-tale
Text, blessing a skin with a god-given
Gospel, gracing a garment
With a gift of words?

A Private Anniversary

In memory of the man who wrote under the name Max Nomad

Warren Hope

They weren't left here by a party hack,
These long-stemmed roses strewn on Marx's grave:
I visualize a withered man, but brave,
Who rents a little box in Tooting Bec.

The box is lined with shelves for note and book:
A door placed on two files forms a desk
Where towering notecards shape an arabesque
Of crimes the bourgeois scholars overlook.

A window lets him glimpse crowds in the street.
He knows he does not love the cut-rate mass —
The long-haired boys with eyes like small dead fish,
The girls who'd think Class War's a punk-rock hit,

Much less their plodding parents, stupefied
By the state's crooked games of work and war,
By their own dreams of pleasure, gin, a whore —
Who cheer each time a saviour's crucified.

And yet he would not serve the ruling class
For all their benefits and pension plans:
He was not born to clap on paper chains
And shuffle at the bidding of a boss.

He has become, perhaps, a class of one,
Maintaining solidarity with ghosts,
One of the lost, living among lost hosts
Who will not usher in a revolution

And that, he can admit, is just as well:
"To think we might have bashed skulls and spilled blood,
Convinced the cause we served was just and good,
Only to make a replica of hell."

Still, on this private anniversary
He takes the Underground to Camden Town,
Seeks out a florist's shop, and then walks on
Until he stands in Highgate Cemetery:

He does not say a word or make a move
And yet the moment is a celebration,
A kind of atheist's commemoration
Of what it means to have known faith and love:

A futile ritual, a silly act
By a crouched figure in a workman's cap:
A gentle creature in a grotesque trap
Who's kept the sense that life is sweet intact.

Examples for Creative Writers

Glyn Hughes

1. Sonnet

Through swamps of doubt that supposedly
are fertile for poets I dreamed of an arcade
of writers sorry for themselves.
One, honoured for his sycophancy,
was as a poet doomed.
One's fatal thought was, is it worth it?
One forgot how to dance, one was silenced by the times,
and one whose character is priapic hubris
wrote doggerel like this to his much-vaunted muses.

I sometimes read their poems in the night
but mostly they stay sealed inside their cases
before... who was it said
that poetry, like love, is best made in bed?

2 Villanelle

Old poets with few verses left to write
when words are hard to find (like breath)
sit in public houses getting tight

their careers abandoned to a consuming night
ungraced by faith.
Old poets with few verses left to write.

dreaming of a late flowering to set right
their gladness of crusts, their ruth,
sit in public houses getting tight.

I bring from the bar my own dark glass of doubt
(alcohol elates pain into poetry) and sit with
old poets with few verses left to write.

Caught at the end without redemption or light —
it could be better, could death,
than old poets with few verses left to write
sitting in public houses getting tight.

A Celebration

Chris Jones

Our day-old boy grizzles in bed
so we shush in turn over his puckered head

as though we fill up shiny balloons
to blow across the threshold of this room

and out the window: picture notes
above the schoolyard *do re mi fa so...*

dots shadowing hills and reservoirs,
a fly-past of cities' frozen squares.

Think how stragglers on wet shingle point and wave
at this blue flock clearing the bay.

In our dreams balloons tangle in nets of trawlers,
are buzzed by fighter jets, drift and fall

on towns loaned out to rain and darkness,
settle on the gold leaves of a forest.

Alaska for Example

From *Into the Blue* by Tony Horwitz

Richard Kell

Tugged again, the rod bends.
He reels another salmon,
fillets it on the beach,
tosses waste to the bald eagles.
Questioned, he speaks tersely,
soon of himself, his "goddamn problems".

Once, Russians from Kamchatka,
greedy for furs, coerced the natives,
took women and children hostage,
wiped out rebels with guns.

Cook, coming in peace, was met
with uneasy deference, kayaker
doffing his cap and bowing
to show he'd learned European manners,
offering as credentials
a Russian receipt for tax.

Mariner Samwell, poet from Wales,
bought sex with a little tobacco,
pigged very lovingly while a husband
lay close to his Wife and her Paramour.

America bought Alaska.
Japanese (World War II)
sent many Aleuts to camps
back in their own country.
U.S. interned the rest "for their protection".
Later apologized,
compensated the few survivors.

During a king-crab boom at Unalaska,
deckhands risked for big money
mutilation or death
from ice, waves, clobbering pots.
Blew thousands of bucks in the Elbow Room
on alcohol, drugs, cards.
Bar brawls raged. Hurled bodies
lay bleeding out in the snow.

Fur, then whales, then gold, then oil,
then crab, halibut, pollock. Yet to come
nothing but empty fathoms
and ice melted by global warming.

Silent, he casts again
while salmon jump from cold grey water
and the bald eagles swoop.

Mountains rise behind the harbour,
"majestic, still unspoiled".

Trizonia

Angela Kirby

O most excellent donkey who,
having never heard of the sleep button,
woke me three times this morning
with your ancient and execrable lament,
do you bemoan the start
of your over-burdened day
and the end of your brief night's rest
in this unpromising patch of scrub
or do you, perhaps, grieve for me
who today must leave this incomparable islet
where there are neither cars
nor motorcycles, where nothing
very much happens, apart
from the occasional birth or marriage
and the rather more frequent deaths,
where there is little to see, just Iannis
repainting the peeling mermaid
on his taverna, and his grandmother
taking a broom to the six hollow-ribbed cats
who have stolen yet another chicken-leg,
and the three old men who,
having finished their backgammon
and the last of the ouzo, now take
the sun's path home across the harbour
in a boat as blue as that clump of scabious
you are considering?

Piano Tuner

Angela Leighton

Who is this man who listens? whose fingers crouch and call,
spanning small frequencies: the tilt of a tremor, the nerve-

centre of a note that hangs on nothing but itself? What
is the measure of this palpable reach, temper, touch-listening,

as if an ear to an ear could suddenly hear itself ring,
and crosswired lyric run, on air, easy as anything?

One, by one, by one, from nuts and bolts, from tacks,
strings, wrest-pins, by force, by hand, he draws each note,

sussing it out, from tusk, tree, root-nerve, growth-rings,
each jointed rod's retort, knee-jerk reaction, hammer-

blows' softened blows like news delivered gently.
Is it an entry to the underworld? Is it the soul?

Or workers' things, articulate joinery, bone and skin,
toolkits of hand, brain, ear-willing bodywork?

The bolted string shivers in its pin, biassed, taut.
A sound hangs in the hang of it. It fills the room,

as if a ghost has come again, in parts, in pieces,
frequent, keeping appointments with us, visiting.

I listen in. Spirit of anvil, hammer, stirrup,
moving spirit — somewhere, far back, we feel by it:

that tuning, wrench to true, a hand's reflex,
the pitched tremor of a branch the bird has left.

Auden at his Villa on Ischia

Herbert Lomas

The poet's still closeted with his talent,
even in the open air. Harassed, wry,
would be-relaxed, martini in hand, he'd
like to give it a holiday.

He won't be happy till its screaming stops,
and that won't happen till he's drunk and smoked
him and his talent to a good death.
His face is the map of its wigglings:

journeys of the soul on an old stone
it's his job to decipher. Meanwhile he keeps
reminding himself to keep on time,
run his accounts straight, and his talent lets him —

provided he gives it breakfast very early
and devotes a day to it. Even then it needs coddling:
the crosswords, the mysteries,the anagrams
that help the thing to overcome its tantrums.

The talent's perfectly fair: all it wants
is total attention. Get that, and it can be patient.
If it screws his muscles, never lets up,
it does offer bliss when he's been good to it:

an ecstasy — what ordinary mortals
ordinarily feel at weekends, out
fishing, or with nothing
particularly to worry about.

John Clare in Burleigh Park

Tom Lowenstein

Under the great oak
I fell and slept
between the roots
curld like a chrysalis.

Dreamt of hedges
filld with songbirds nests
the ink splashd eggs
with orange and vermilion
burns on single blue.

I heard the red mite
climbing the green bark,
the female beetle
shuffling her shards

and by my ear
beneath the root
the pupa writhe
between the stones.

The sun rose white
as a winter moon,
and woke me
shivering with Rime.

Revaluation in the Poets' Pub

Alexis Lykiard

Our cheerful group debates the "worst Poetic Crime",
bent on linking
offender and sad lines, as hindsight often shows
how some dead poetaster ended second-rate.
The bubbles in the glass keep winking,
threaten to spill into most splendid rhyme,
enrich us, help us laugh at penury we chose.
Each vows, mock-serious, to sing and praise perfection,

shun the hour of karaoke, chase perception
until the bland finale — unforgiving Close
of Play. Forget good work, if keen to cultivate
contacts, sell out, or flatter for a fee.
Best stay content to struggle honestly,
enjoying the hard game of poetry...
Careerists all betray their slender gifts. You name
one such who compromised the sacred flame,

was duly celebrated, soon and late.
Born charmer, lovely chap, too smooth to hate —
how fortunate the fellow-travelling apostate
should end up safely Faberized, Possum's old mate!
Ignorant of what cash the CIA
can freely freight the verbal scales with, he drew pay,
scarcely self-questioning: the dull dog had his day.
Thus did a disingenuous, well-connected creep

engender verse whose very bathos might seem deep.
Tall story man or Thirties schoolboy-pretender?
Banal white knight of the soul, Sir Stephen Spender
was a talent surrendered to Caesar, one long lifetime
spent in thinking
"continually of those
who were truly great."

The Way to Go

Clare MacDonald Shaw

Six bikers get themselves shot. Astride chrome,
helmets underarm, they snap each other on the street,
not up some hairpin bend, heroic.

Unlikely backdrop — windows selling quilts, pots,
waxy Drizabones for shepherds. Border village
creeps uphill, houses close as teeth,

but there's a gap, black hole in the wall.
Final offer: lose your wheels and go,
here to hereafter with the PURPLE FUNERAL CO.

Cheaper singles to the underworld?
Drop out, high on jazz, or book morrismen
with hats and staves to step-hop by your hearse.

Don't sign for slow-burn C of E.
Our green canoes will float you down the Styx
with a plaster cat for company,

so quit the circuit, motorway, Route 101,
and get off-road down under. The bikers
choose a coffin, pose (Dracula rising),

rev and vanish, living for speed.
High Street shivers with noise,
blinking glass in the sun;

flakes of lead paint slip down a crack.
Now Mr Lock's feet start their work —
daily spirals out of town, looping green lanes,

threading them together, beating the bounds.
Miles off he sits on verges, just clear
of skidding wheels. He's been drawn and hung

as *Mr L in the Rain*. Oils distil him
out of light and wet, treading puddled tracks
by Offa's Dyke; tin barns keep rusting red.

Cloudbreak; a hedge soaks through canvas;
drops magnify green pores. In the flesh
he gets our seasons going. Pilewort stars

burnt out, his eye turns speedwell into campion.
He tests the hot stink of a meadowsweet ditch,
bombed by gnats. May his late fall not sprout

lilies in cellophane and stiff chrysanths.
Our ritual's wrong; better a mound
under elder than slabbed on Marble Row,

but space is finite here. So get in the purple
transit van, indulge your passing fancy,
Wave a bunch of bright weeds at crowds

of absent friends; don't pay for that
old clock bell and impromptu blackbird.
Exit in a lightning flash, easy to fix.

Dancing at Home in the Thirties

Mairi MacInnes

They rolled back the rugs to reveal the plain boards
which they sprinkled with crystals to make a smooth floor,

trod them in and then seized each other and swooped,
glided, out of character, the pair of them sharing a mood,

breathily humming or murmuring the words of a song
dancing by themselves without music, so I had to make fun

of them both to myself and ran off embarrassed and hid.
I don't know what else happened or what they did,

only, the rugs were replaced when I came in again,
and they were laughing and humming right up to the evening.

So later that night, after the guests came and they'd dined,
rugs were rolled back again, and music unwound

from seventy-eights on our box of a gramophone
and all danced, transformed, the women in their slinky long

dresses, the men in their black tailored suits, white
shirts, bow ties, rosetted shoes, elastic-sided boots

just visible from the top of the stair as they whirled,
portly Bill Brown and Nell, slim Alan, Rita, Dan, Andrea.

In the morning — Sunday of course — my parents slept late.
A smell of cigars downstairs, ash in the grate,

the furniture still pushed against the walls,
the maids bustling. I started to dance by myself

till Betty whirled me about. No, let me alone,
I protested: I wanted to dance by myself, quite alone.
(I was little, you understand, I didn't know anything.)

Autographs

Jamie McKendrick

Basil D'Oliveira and John Barbirolli,
the black man in white and the white man in black,
were the only signatures I had stuck into
my signature book. Little interested me less
than watching cricket except perhaps watching music,
but I liked the two names that were a secret rhyme
like almost acrostics. Because of his colour,
because he was a "half-caste" and did off-spins
and most likely with him with us we would win,
the South Africans had stopped D'Oliveira
playing, which meant the end of the whole tour.
This must have been Old Trafford, 1960-something.
Barbirolli was playing at home, away for me,
with the Manchester Hallé Orchestra.
Was Hallé French for hello or for halo?

Sir John Barbirolli hello would you sign this
(scrunched-up programme) please? He swept his coat tails
athletically round to face me as though he'd
gladly knock everyone else and everything over,
but like the wrist-roll of an elegant square-cut
he'd timed his coat-trail to a T
in that cramped backstage dressing-room
brimming with champagne and congratulations.
D'Oliveira and Barbirolli smiled elatedly
as if handing on a bat or a baton,
unaware they'd bestowed their attention
on a keck-handed, tone-deaf imposter
who wasn't collecting signatures anyway,
who just happened to be standing in the right place
and was then pushed forwards with a pen and paper.

Ballad of Robert Johnson

Edward Mackinnon

The Old Man was on the loose
Looking for to do some harm
On his way to Robinsonville
From the Parchman prison farm

Tunica County in '29,
Ginny Travis, Robert's bride
Was all of sixteen years old
When she and their baby died

Robert played the levee camps
Calletta treated him kind
But Blind Lemon had given him a notion
He had rambling on his mind

Wasn't cut out to be a sharecropper
He had rambling on his mind

The Old Man hummed a tune
Blues falling down like hail
Smiled and said to himself
I'll put a hellhound on his trail

Soon as Robert left the plantation
There was a hellhound on his trail!

The hound caught him in Greenwood
At a jookhouse near the town
God help him, Son and Charley
God help him, Willie Brown

He met a little queen of spades
He'd always been fancy free
Her husband ran that roadhouse show
Robert wouldn't let her be

She was sweeter than Jumpin' Judy
And he wouldn't let her be

Robert thought of jelly roll
Thought he could shake it all night long
But there was strychnine in his whisky
And man, that brew was strong

He was buried by the county
On a narrow piece of ground
Near a withered little rosebush
With dry weeds all around

The Old Man said to himself
As his hound began to whine
"I can do what the hell I like
Below the Jim Crow line"

"I can do what the hell I like",
he laughed, "Below the Jim Crow line"

Flugel

Paul McLoughlin

for Dick Pearce

What happened to the flugelhorn
you always played, that had you
turn down trumpet gigs, the famous
brother too brash, too much
like the army that could not
sustain itself on minor modal scales?

Did you buy yourself out, grow
your hair, practise, practise, find
the melting, mellow sound of
private life less trumpet loud, play
the fatter horn, because it caught
a quieter, self-effacing mood?

You were never one for soaring
high, preferring Miles to Dizzy
any day, Rollins to Bird. Is it
because bewildered in a world
you can't believe you helped create,
you must speak louder now?

So many lack technique, can only
marvel at a winged horn that puffs
the air with proof that gentle rain
can slake a giant thirst. Did it grow
too comfortable, so much the salve
you locked away its charm for good?

As if suddenly you were a sophist
duping those who'll follow any lure
that takes them out beyond the boom
of modern gods towards the human
birdsong that's heartsease if only
temporarily, then temporarily at least.

In Crombie Again

John Manson

I

We were late in leaving Aberdour
where we missed the tide to Inchcolm
No one had bothered to look it up
Now in a minibus with strange colleagues
we are driving fast through the ancient lands of Crombie
part of the shire of Culross, in stooks again
trying to catch up the time
to spend an educational half-hour in Culross
half an hour in Culross
where every stone has a history
We are driving above Limekilns
the Gellet Rock, the King's Cellars, the Ghauts
We are driving above Charlestown
the planned village, the sutlery, the kilns, the caves
We are driving above Crombie
Kirk, Point, Place, Pier.

II

Not so in the autumn three years earlier
When we were getting to know each other
Meeting by accident, wilful accident
Nervous arrangements
On our best behaviour
Feeling our way

Heat out of the day
The ripening of growth
Taking in the corn
The thresh of sheaves forked on the load
Now the hum of the motor

Shiver in the air
Shiver in me.

Labour of Love

André Mangeot

Somewhere, against odds, they endure —
Holding the line against doom-mongers, grant-cuts, bookstore
Or festival lockouts — up at dawn with strong coffee,
Eager for the desk — typescript and proof — Brahms or Mingus
Swirling, eerie paradigms, through the house. Margins fill with
Tuh! — Surely not! — Is he joking? — instinct for candour,
Rhythm and music, form beyond words. And sometimes,
Insistent from the slush-pile, the real thing —
No froth or posturing, calm and clear, its own voice.
Garnering the tick that means, finally, "Yes" —

In the post the hurried man's semi-legible scrawl,
Sweetest music of all to those versed in the brush-off —

"Late next-autumn... will happily publish..."
Unlike any feeling or subsequent moment, this first
Confirmation — independent, respected — of one's chosen course.
And how many now have embarked with the same imprimatur?
Small-press lighthouse, Beeston powerhouse — spun on a shoestring!

Begin with the Letter "S"

Nancy Mattson

ASK AT the corner of Cross and Upper
Streets for directions to Sadler's Wells.
CHEW AN answer: "Where dancers fly
Near the Round Pond that gathered fresh
Water from Myddelton's New River,
Artfully dug with the backing of James I,
King and patron of purity in
English scripture and drinking water that
Serpentines over thirty-nine miles from
Hertfordshire's sweet sources — only
Twenty miles on a crow's back, but the
Admirable Myddelton fixed his jeweller's

Eye on every inch in the contour lines
Above or below a hundred feet,
Keeping his river level but gyratory,
Never straight." A pause for breath
Staunches the overflow of words,
Allows the London visitor time to think,
Hail a taxi, with luck, arrive for
Act Two of *Petrushka* by the Kirov.
What else would a local historian give?
Straight answers? Pigs might dance. Poor you, no
Closer to ballet at Sadler's Wells
Than to tangos in rectangular Saskatchewan.

Say, what's the point of these
Anagrams anyway? Poetry's
Serious business, like seeding flax.
Keep it real, we want
Archetypes and heartbreak.
Toss out your word tricks,
Concentrate on nature, give us epics,
Hard times, love and elegies:
Everyone works and dies and mourns.
We don't hold with sneaky little
Acrostics in these parts, no sirree,
Not in the solid heart of Saskatchewan.

O Lucky Man

Philip Mead

We didn't think about the works so much as the literary
    times
zithery, Japanese sirens seemed to insist: back your
    imagination
disappear into your own handicraft as a happy pilgrim
the emperor will be astonished and you'll get to inhabit
your seasonal allegory, the opposite of film, a careless scroll
a welter of subjects stretching out beyond the watery rooftops
tracer lines of traffic noise arcing through the monochrome
background. Suddenly we realised the irrelevance of
psychology, or its essential incompatibility with the world
what kind of methods are available, anyway, for tragic views?
It's irresponsible but I just wanted to cavort through
    the scenes
getting lost in the stacks, joining the tableaux in Strawberry
    Fields
with a soundtrack by Alan Price, ideally
that's hardly asking for a quinquereme of Nineveh!
Lots has happened though, the family continues to change
a bright, twirling salad announces itself in the titles
a strange distortion has fallen across all official things
just as when Gerry Hall spins her tail in that glamrock clip.
I remember the day as heedless, like the sun
you carried your notebook with the silver hair.
There was the bathtub with its enormous brass taps
one of those things outside contemporary scales of living
a reminder that in the time of nations all perspectives were
    hand-held
he was never without language for its companionship
his sandal-shoon, a heart for every fate
without him it was a reticulum, blankly revenant in
labels like "Lord Byron's Boxing Gloves"

an unblotted fluency growing up somehow in the chilly
neo-Gothic passages, those always amazingly neat papers!
even more striking than the Orientalia
and/or the wonderful bells of lead
fun with waterworks around the repurposed Abbey
a good head for money, even a memory for hotels
above all a Franciscan care for creatures and friends
"I'm looking forward to a quiet night in my dressing-gown."
Imagine a tender, second-generation Romantic holding down
a summer semester as a media intern!
all day on a vinegary sounding word like "operational".
Notwithstanding the "nineteenth-century" poses on
    snowy pinnacles
the dedicated, continental brothel trawling
he intuited how the perilous roads go, the wintry nights
the uncontrollable tone of most sentences, even the gift shop.
He spoke like that in his mind, a doer not a Sensitive Plant
dread, fathomless, alone, disappearing
naked across a neatly drawn field with plumes of smoke
in a small green vale called Tempe, a perspective of utopia
perhaps, next to the overpasses and the shipping lanes
intent on evading even the subtlest coercions of morality
a meanderer in the polar, editorialising regions
his influence widening like a martini glass! you wish
that's a beautiful thing, the language of inquiry
lossy compression, getting to choose one's own mode of
mediation, calling all those with a predilection for freedom
was that really a fox strolling across the back lawn?
Others might look uncomprehendingly at finding solace
in a chapter on refactory rhyming and
monumental oddities dropping out of the orphic fountain's
side like a string of allied paratroopers, literally
Ipecacuanha lozenges for Julianna?
Life is too often stripped of its pleasantness
by the steps of false assumption
it's roaring with pain outside, as
Marge lets Norah see Sharon's telegram.
Sad to say people tend not to live in the past any more

least of all historical novelists, I mean really
everyone's bound up in their own self-expression
only the very few are doing something properly enjoyable
like growing wasabi plants in southern Tasmania
or searching for a cure for science.
Everyone's a failure, that's our role
whatever's possible belongs to the half of art that's fleeting
and fathers in their sober prose accounts are dysfunctional
for the most part we maintain a positive tone
only occasionally drawn into thinking about the turbid
    depths of
the estuary, the way young reporters used to show up
    at the door
looking for material to write about, following what
people did in a genuinely delighted way
call me old-fashioned, but what were those stereotypical
petals floating down into Verlaine's glass of pilsener?
a Harvard Square poem by Orson Welles?
an origami fold in the cinematic scene?
Whatever it was, it was swirling.
Looking back through the drawers of diaries and letters
it's hard to know how to make sense of the material
those that had their selves wiped of all signs like a
whiteboard, those who married in the end and had kids
those who went to live on an outer island with the
    multimedia artists
over time, in some measure, reckless love turns the hands
    into claws
small lives take on the pattern of kohl-eyed monographs
convergence seems to be happening everywhere
which is unfortunate, unless there's some secret message
I'm not getting, the entertainment value of work is saddening
as you always suggested. What can you do? Cigarette life.
We're hanging around, waiting on a jpeg from Sylvie and
    Bruno
who're in Japan where the transit system maps are in 3-D
and things are either animate or inanimate, like a real
    piece of art.

For John Lucas

Stanley Middleton

How should I greet so learned
A man? Like his old cricket captains with
Question, quick answer. "I'd like... would you open
The bowling?" "Where?" "Top end." The myth
Of age has not yet touched him; seventy
Years old he'd still rap bails and fingers,
Dust powder off pads. He claws
So much from life; literature leaps and lingers
At his shrewd eye. He sharpens our dullness,
Convinces us to search the ancient laws, pell-mell
As now we dash for newer fangled codes. We speak
To him in awe. Friendly he starts to tell
A dozen views he's learnt that day. His verse,
Style finely worked, digs deep for gold
In games, strong youthful trivia, flute-
Music, jazz, Romania, death. He's never sold
Us short, but spilt our tears
With flooding sorceries of words, which tote
Us poor near his high miracles
Of rich simplicity. A quick friend wrote
To me some weeks ago that he'd
Had poems taken by <u>Saint</u>
John. I wish I'd thought
Of that. His apocalypses mayn't
Only colour our small lives, but trumpet
Larger encouragements. Here he stands,
Up-dated saint, like seaside sunshine ordering
Shadows away from our night-darkened lands.

Fats

John Mole

Hammer those spatulate
ringed fingers, run

the vertiginous keyboard's
length, a thumbnail

gliss, then chase
the accident, the chancy

modulation, grin
at each gain revealed

by loss, throw back
that massive head, become

pure joy, the love-struck
face of it, a kid again

to pump your pedal car
along its track of sound

while all the others step aside
to send you round the block,

then home in triumph
to the here, the now,

the leap to your applause
in bulk made nimble by the light

of music, in the shimmy
of your outsize suit,

and mercy, mercy
where did you get those shoes?

At Readers Bridge

Hubert Moore

It's what you don't expect yet know
must be, the mild descent through willows,
the small flat bridge, and below,

when you stop at the rail and lean,
words going briskly under,
not book-by-book, but in-

divisible, the body of the whole
of literature, eddies, ripples,
currents, undercurrents, all

one flowing thing. Note how a ticket
for a football match floats
at the very point we've got to.

Grange Boy

Blake Morrison

Horse-chestnuts thudded to the lawn each autumn.
Their spiked husks were like medieval clubs,
Porcupines, unexploded mines. But if
You waited long enough they gave themselves up —
Brown pups, a cow opening its sad eye,
The shine of the dining-room table.

We were famous for horse-chestnuts. Boys
From the milltown would ring at our door asking
Could they gather conkers and I'd to tell them
Only from the ground — no stick-throwing.
I watched from the casement as they wandered
In shadow, trousers crammed like mint-jars.

One morning they began without asking.
Plain as pikestaffs, their hurled sticks filleted
Whole branches, the air filled like a pillowfight
With rebellion and leaves. I was alone.
I had not father's booming voice. They were free
To trample through our peaceable estate.

Afterwards, matching father in a show
Of indignation (bloody vandals and thugs)
I imagined their home ground: the flagged backyards,
The forbidden alleys and passages
Winding up and out on purple moor,
The coal-sacks glistening in locked sheds.

It is June now, the chestnut scattered
Like confetti. He summoned me today
To the billiard-room — that incident
With an apprentice. *I've told you before.*
A son in your father's firm, you're looked to
For an example. I don't know what to do.

So I sit at my rosewood desk, lines fading
Across the parkland. I've been getting pamphlets
In a plain brown envelope and feel like
A traitor. Strangers have been seen
By the wicket-gate. Mother keeps to her bed.
English, we hoard our secrets to the end.

Jihad

Graham Mort

Don't ask me if this is my friend's enemy or my enemy's
friend, this fox with its fanatic eyes slinking at stone walls
where conifers drape the dark and dip in restless breaths
of wind; this fox with nose held high to gauge each nuance
of the gloom, head lasered by its own bright stare.

Drizzle smokes in the headlights, the engine pants. I've
braked the car but the fox won't move. Its coat is brown
in the rain, not red the way a fox is in a storybook or fable.
Its tail is carried low to scuff away tracks through larch
needle humus of the night-time woods.

The radio brings *a new kind of war* — tells me why the West
is dangered now, though I don't get uniqueness here when
war is death and death is old. Wipers bleat and whirr,
    smearing
glass, stretching a film of oil to a thinning lie. Then that
tune I can't forget: *I get along without you very well*, its

unsung words keeping time with blades on a windscreen
wet with rain. Insinuations of the night hold me here in the
fox's unironic mullah's glare. He walks away, slips me to
his memory of vixen musk and other kills: a whiff of petrol,
a blurred face, the engine's rasping breath, pale hands at

the wheel which he allows to pass. No more. He'll watch the
pricked blood of my taillights dwindle, the plantation
    shoulder
its cape of dark, rain needle undergrowth, embroidering its
fatal text. The fox hurdles headlines, finesses frequencies,
rides that song in his own breaking wave of fear.

His gaze returns to spike false sleep where I turn in
half truths, half remembered. Now pausing, now sniffing
the larch-scented night, ears pricked, brush stiffening, all
senses turning in that gimballed head to lock onto the
hare upwind that hasn't yet imagined it must die.

Spring

Michael Murphy

You can't interpret, little less translate
the fuse of spring where it is lit
among the dead: shards of glass cemented
above backyard gates, the apocalypse
of an empty coke can in the gutter,
the aimless trash that goes flutter-

ing out of sight, out of mind. It whispers
like a Rembrandt angel, stooping
at the ear of an evangelist
who, seeing his clouded vision lift and clear,
knows this moist warm breath
is prayer, substantive as a knot in air.

Wordless, fallible, commensurate,
not knowing why or how, he starts to write.

Shoestring Shuffle

Variation on lines by John Heath-Stubbs

Helena Nelson

The unpredictable lay in his arms
in a tender and unquiet rest;
he breathed in deep and held it,
keeping the new note fast

aching aloud and high and low
for joy of the unknown thing,
trusting his own true element,
source of a human spring

inescapably coursing,
restlessly sweet and strong,
unquiet improvisation
on an old, old song.

Henry James

Robert Nye

Henry James, top hat in hand, important, boring,
Walks beautifully down the long corridor
Of the drowned house just off Dungeness
At the turn of the century. It is 3pm probably.
It is without doubt October. The sun decants
Burgundy through high windows. The family portraits
Are thirteen versions of the one face, walking
On the thick trembling stalk of Henry James.
It is a face which looks like the face of a goldfish
Fed full of breadcrumbs and philosophy, superbly
Reconciled to its bowl. The difference
Between Henry James and a goldfish, however,
Is that Henry James has nostrils. Those nostrils observe
An exquisite scent of evil from the library.
Henry James goes beautifully on his way. His step
Is complicated. (He nurses an obscure hurt. It is this
Which kept him from active service in the sex war.)
Listen and you will hear the trickle of his digestive juices–
Our author has lunched, as usual, well–
Above the sweetly unpleasant hum of his imagination.
His shoes make no squeak and he deposits no shadow
To simplify the carpet. Henry James
Turns a corner. Henry
James meets Henry
James. Top hat, etcetera. Henry James
Stops. Henry James stares. Henry James
Lifts a moral finger. "You again!"
He sighs. "How can you be so obvious?"
Henry James blushes and Henry James flees and Henry
James goes beautifully on his way, top hat
In hand, important, boring, he walks down
The long life-sentence of his own great prose.

Apricots

Ruth O'Callaghan

were scarce that year
but jalapeno chillies tumbled
from rush baskets, sprawled
on marble slabs in downtown
tavernas where 'roaches ran
or lay with wrinkled beans
in an earthenware pot
on the Aegean peninsula:
Panos placed pieces on his bar,
patrons scooped whole handfuls —
metaxa diminished the difference
between tears and rain.

A flush of early peppers waited
to welcome the striped bass
battered in sea sweat
that Yannis would bring
in the absence of orchids

Royal Oak

George Parfitt

Small room; and voices from the bar.
Just four of us here:
a pair of young men playing cards
quietly, for pints and pennies,
saying little, easing a week's work
into the peace of small bets and warm beer.

From his corner, where his feet have worn the lino,
Big Bob has just taken them for a pint of brown,
product of patient, blunt hinting,
masterwork of crude accretion,
climax of impervious intervention
on their peaceful comradeship.

We've sat across this room for years,
Bob and I; through strange estrangements.
But usually we've talked, to no effect,
sealed in our pasts and in the fears
of different views and cultures.
Now filling-up time arrives:

Wall-eyed Brian, in suit and bow-tie.
His fake-blonde consort, black dress
with silver trimmings. She's well down time's slope,
but holding on, coping with the sphinx of age.
I'm drawn to snobbish satire, but a burst
of bawdy gossip, blank assertions
draws me back to a kind of awe.

Sans Souci Park

Tom Paulin

The last big war it's
got under the skin of this house
here the scrimped and the saved
— newspapers tin cans bottles
brown paper (creased) bits of string
an odd furry
hot water bottle chewed by moths
keep the house
— oh some empty cardboard boxes—
keep the house
on its always steady course
for in truth — really
it's a cold water flat
among several flats on two levels
where old people live stealthily
quite naturally in the same stucco house
a house I want to call Ballykinlar
(place of the candlestick)
after the camp and the barracks
under the Mourne Mountains
— hardly palatial that name
— I mean Ballykinlar —
and your flat it's chilled
by utility furniture
and the saved electric
furniture that says that's that
end of story finis
as we eat our meal
under the kitchen clotheshorse
(its cloth and woolly blade
hangs from the ceiling above our heads)
which — cloth cap maybe —

which brings back that private
squaddie from the Gorbals —
you tried to save from the gallows
a poor shopkeeper he'd raided
— raided and pushed —
banged his head and died
— a few weeks later
(winter of 43)
Mr Justice Pierrepoint tied the noose
— we need neither of us think
of that nameless kid
trying to eat his last breakfast
— as — I won't to be polite
call this prog or a feed — as
we start on our meal
a single lamb shank with a few
scraps of onion and carrot
— baked in a low heat
along with some biscuit and parkin
to a recipe that's about as
basic as a ration card
— ration card or a boat deck— boat
with some cargo
braving the tide bar
like that ship in the bottle
or your too tired face
there at the window

Reading Lawrence in Beeston

Heather Peace

My great-great-granny bought her flour
At the Eastwood Co-op;
She couldn't read a book or write her name.

> Among the leafmould of my teenage years
> Lie *Sons and Lovers* and *Women in Love* —
> Dost *know*? Dost *feel*? Dost *yearn*?

> His words made my heart resound
> Like a tuning fork
> Before it knew the meaning of music.

The fourth generation —
She'd never have believed it —
Finds its way to university.

> My hopes were high when I arrived in seventy-five;
> To my amazement they all scorned the academic pleb
> Who legged it with the French professor's wife.

> Some snobs had gone, but several lingered on;
> The establishment still ruled
> In Snotingham.

What matter if a novel's long and too intense,
If it bursts corsets and frees folk like us? Who gives
    a shit
If he's not posh, nor gay, nor stayed to earn his wages
    down the pit?

> We had good teachers, John was one;
> Subversive currents lapped the corridor.
> Truth and beauty waving, drowning, noisily reborn.

Turns out fashion matters more than truth and
Anyhow, DHL means
Something altogether different now.

Plain and simple words express a heart that's true,
And handsome is as handsome does
As all my grannies used to say, and do.

Oval Tests, End of Summer

Nigel Pickard

Time and time again,
the quickness of it,
those spun-out shadows,
in the declaring sun.

Too Many Ends in View

Christopher Pilling

My trainer laces are far too long.
If I cut them short I'll lose two ends
And still have four. I'm frayed and blasting
At tbe prospect. I could go barefoot, casting
The trainers to kingdom come. He who sends
Things there hasn't an earthly, however strong.

One ties oneself in knots to do hardly a thing.
I turn for consolation to John but he's got
Going with lively jazzy chords — the iron's hot —
And planning miracles with shoestring!

Two Tots of Irish

Richard Poole

1. Duet

I was sat out on the lawn.
The sun was playing hide and seek
among the sheep grazing on heaven.
The flies were legion, the blackbird sleek.

The grass was freshly cut
and, though its odour's not that of a rose
(less of the princess, more of the slut),
it was emerald in my nose.

On my lap, Paul Muldoon
lay unread by me and my ticklers —
the flies dancing a rigadoon
on the salt-licks of my fingers.

The bird and I whistled *Sonata
for Garden Gnome and Court Jester.*

2. The Stile

As I sat reading a Heaney sonnet
on a plank of the trackside stile between
Llandanwg and Pensarn, the two-fifteen
clattered past and the sun doffed its bonnet
of cloud. Now things could really wear their colours —
white the swans, green the marsh-moss, black
the rich mud of the ditch walls and the bladderwrack
on the bridge-rails, blue the estuarial waters.

I'd like to be drinking light and retsina
just like Heaney, in Greece, for there's nothing
Arcadian here — unless you count the cows lazing
beyond the blackthorn, full-cudded. Light is meaner
here, tight-fisted, terra firma watery —
oozy and seepy as it leaks into the sea.

Lines for an English Heine

Peter Porter

I

Our monosyllables are fraught
with all the things we cannot say,
And feeling now is drawn to thought
While thought is threadbare with delay.

The street of houses built secure
Has one side only — opposite
The railway walls raised to immure
The sky are secretly moonlit.

Germanic hopes by tongue-tied lake
In simple language trail the heart,
But English words cannot awake
From secrecy a speaking art.

II

The land is out at sea; we mean
The dead are breaking on the land,
Their lives once like the waves between
The flooding and the drying sand.

On beaches soft philosophers
Learn hardness as their minds entail
Some danger where no movement stirs
On empty shell or drifting sail.

Or were they seeking continents
Drowned years ago whose merchants thought,
As veterans of immanence,
That cargoes would come safe to port?

III

I stand here now where once she stood,
Two girls in tow, our daughters who,
So well-behaved, so tamed to good,
Each one hand at a time withdrew.

My sight must conjure from a space
The person in this bald graveyard;
I touch but cannot see her face,
The same stern angels standing guard

Of whom she scarcely felt aware
Being so close to where they rule.
One is the number of despair
And aggregate of ridicule.

IV

A self-indulgent dreamer
Or so his fellows thought
Whose visions of completeness
Are what is sold and bought.

Yet he too bought and traded
In civil wish and hope,
His black world reinvaded
By blatant heliotrope.

Thus, in his dreamscape pictured,
The sun, that spectrum'd yell,
Could stream through death's tight fingers
And light, the plains of hell.

Greek February and Then...

Philip Ramp

Greek February, now there's something built for long
    remembering.
More than winter, less than spring.
The oddest of harmonies where months of seeming death
    awake accomplished
and set nature burgeoning, blossoming almond trees,
    virgin light squeezed
from the season's failing dark, the olives discreetly fading
    in behind them,
in essence mocking any season's worth, their silver-
    coated leathery green
that sheds time's corrosive drops like any other rain.
February in Greece is marked by all the changes
my later northern spring demands, and as clearly seen
but the subtlety of the massive, total change
that makes each moment over from the ground up,
    nearly identical but never quite,
though so clear, is lost on me here, even in conception;
all I know is antiquity with its few small gestures comes
    sweeping back:
the hills are suddenly purple, the sea black; I see in
    summary, the apogee.

I *do* remember spring's first day last year because it
    came on time
and like time does sometimes: all at once, (another
    summary of sorts)
for the murky, lingering browns and greys were erased in
    one buzzing night
and blown over the hills of dawn like so much pollen, sun
    racing after wind,
wind sun-bright, light batted back and forth in the

    clouds, by the clouds,
spring speeding up while time seemed to slow, stumble,
unused to its big cumbersome shoes built for hours
    in the rain,
its huge prints left randomly about the fields,
cookie cutter shapes immediately filled with flowers
    racing up,
that waved beneath the waves of planting birds, waved at
    the green tide
rolling past, the air above them bursting into sea-like
    singing, song learned
if not from sea at least from coming *over* sea, soaring
    high notes,
booming lows, snatched from ancient arias, the sky's
prime blue settling on my head!
Cloth of light shaken out in one long and expert snap;
table ready; and it did *receive*, bountifully,

Three Prentice Pieces

Arnold Rattenbury

In the car-boot sale, a wooden pulpit
large doll's house size, even the silliest
detail exact. "Load of bullshit"
says a glancer-by. But a stander-still,
"That's prentice work. Man, it's brilliant!"

Sixty years back and you could watch
the Master Builders' apprentice pass-outs:
young lads quarter-scaling, from a batch
of blueprints, risers, half-landing, next
three risers, all the bannisters, the rails,
newel; and gawp at youth so expert.
Then the event went missing. Masters
saw no need of the skills, blind bastards.

Here's an eight-sided box: seven
by seven, the height built up in fourteen
half-inch square-cut pieces, uneven
in length but once in each the important
octagon angle. Abutments a miracle:
they did no better blocking the Pyramids!
And glows for the old man now, in this dusk
of skilling, belief, programme, just
those reds-with-darknesses mahogany musters
from love. A keepsake, a tower, a keep
on history's motte. While the people sleep.

Two Flowers

Deryn Rees-Jones

Peony
Such intimacy when I press into the darkness of its
heart,
as if it were a friend of mine
— like love — like death —
I speak to it of this and that, I furnish it with whispers.

Chinese Lanterns
Bright crêpe on summer nights, a carnival,
of melancholy heat, a row of pumpkin-headed smiles.
They're metaphors to wear against the dark,
who wear their loss barefoot,
like sad fluorescent dancers.

On the Mobile

Peter Robinson

Beyond the Lifestyle Protection Centre
there were choices to be made
and ripped grey plastic bags
snagged on the branches of pollarded trees
being dug out round their roots —
no doubt for transplanting to who-knows-where.

'I've got to give him time to fall in love with me,'
said the girl with a mobile at her ear
as she boarded our train for Crewe,
and I was just about to say …

But then we shuddered off from the platform.
Threads of bungalows would fray
in landscapes with seagulls on filter-beds,
ones where my first wife's uncle
commuted to his job with British Rail.

Past willow-herb embankments,
equivocal points and sidings,
it was like she'd given me a moment's pause
to tie up the loose ends of time.

So then those summers seemed all one
missed connection, the betrayal
of more than enough to recall
how little I know about love …

Yet right when you're wondering whatever could happen
in these slight returns of life,
it happens, it suddenly happens
I'm back on my night watchman's nightshift
reading *Hard Times* by the light
of a drinks dispensing machine;

I'm back in some Luna Park, or Disneyland forlorn,
seeing coach windows fill up with her voice
as she gives him time to fall in love
and we pass flaked bridges, pubs, and villas …
It's almost like being reborn.

Counting the Cards

Maurice Rutherford

'The Infant Saviour', 1493
by Albrecht Dürer; Launceston; Gordale Scar;
from 'Chagford through the Ages' — Wendy Mee;
Spain — Barcelona. Greetings from afar

and not so far — The Minster, Beverley
just down the road from here. Titbits of news.
Kowloon; Porthcawl; thatched roofs at Shottery;
more of the same in Cockington; six views

from you-know-where in Greece; Matisse; a Bosch;
'All Greek' by Pauline — vibrant, oil on board;
a bureau by Charles Rennie Mackintosh;
two Canalettos adding to the hoard.

My earliest is postmarked '92,
by Wessily Kandinsky, called 'Blue Sky —
a detail'. *Shoestring* Poem Cards; a few
more gems of art to tease and hold the eye;

Japan — Atami Hot Springs, '94;
the wilderness of St. Columba, Tas.
Aegina once again — blue-painted door
in front of which a sharp-eyed snapper has

immortalized three kittens as they play.
Each valued then, all priceless to this day,
I've totted up, as keen curators do,
repeating "Bestest, John" times eightytwo!

Considering Bridget Riley's
Metamorphosis

Lawrence Sail

Here it is, in black and white —
the optic nerve seduced into playing
a blinder. Pressures out of sight
mill all images back to latency,
the mind's series, treacherous and true.

Yet definitions are at their sharpest
when speeding towards the point where disks
of silver and black throng to the mesh
of something like judgement, then a remix
of tried perceptions, making them new —
as, say, the image of holes in a colander
themselves drained away; or a swarming stream
of fish-eggs; or a geometer's world
of ciphers somehow unhooked from time,
an eternity made of in betweens.

Now you don't see it, now you don't —
the invisible ink which you know is there,
the oxygen of desire, which can't
be denied; that gasp of mortal love, or
the momentary gift of all its meanings.

The Heathrow to Melbourne Flight

Andrew Sant

No better place to reflect when the yolk
moon's at the window, thanks to Qantas
and aerodynamics —
                              a mere day
to travel, book in hand, half way round the planet
and delay rising tax

on the atmosphere and dark forests. To be obedient.
Belted in. Dream a bit, think of how
where you've lived with the neighbours
is now in row 58 your exclusive domain.

To make elbow room prime space
above a desert where there's a track
and the promise of slow traffic. No better way

to save hours. Quite so, as you fly eastward,
your sun implies, rising for the price
of two appearances, three times.

No better place to exercise,
otherwise the celebrity horror, thrombosis,
might make a fuss, even
in first class and prove more expensive.

This, and the endless cuisine, while you're flying
in what seems the world's biggest intestine,
serve to emphasise this is where you now live

and how you wish to continue to do so —
asleep perhaps, or absorbed, during this novel-
length flight, in classic fiction. At one sitting.

Taking the Hexameter for a Walk

Matt Simpson

John, there's only this last half-inch of ouzo left,
a fistful of bivalve pistachios and half
a jar of olives. The tan's long flaked away. *Well*,
your letter asks, *glad to be back?*

Don't remind me! That
roller-coaster taxi to Athens Airport,
the jet's growling up-rush descent to Manchester
over black, snow-daubed Pennine Hills.

So things happened
after I left! Four Spanish women, unexplained,
you met at Katerina's, plus *two Germans and
a villainous-looking man who could have come from
anywhere*, reminding you of Monsieur Rigaud
as Citizen of the World. Then George's name day
celebrated *one day before — this is Greece!* — with
village friends, and one day after this with you, then
with other friends the following!

I'm not surprised,
all those adventitious comings/goings, Fireflies
in Katerina's scented garden that evening
with a foreign Correspondent and the son of
a famous children's author and Katerina
throwing bones to the dogs, and boisterous about
her translations of Pushkin and solemn about Greek
distrust of Albanians. On our walk back
you observed the island was now a-yap with dogs.

And talking of that walk back and fireflies, how can
I forget the unspooky little cemetery
with its exquisite nightlights, moon-glazed white marble,
how sensible it felt walking there at midnight,
breaking our talk of Manley Hopkins to do so,
(Age and age's evils, hoar hair,/Ruck and wrinkle)
then sauntering back to the flat as if life was all
easy-going-natural, the gods not bothered
what we did or spoke of, dogbark keeping at bay
thoughts of scurvy banditry.

                                Now you've discovered
the island's *very best retsina in a shed*
— behind a little store — there on that same road back *—*
where one Maria dispenses wine from a vast
barrel as well as *a superb local read sold*
from a barrow near the church, good enough, you say,
to convert to Greek Orthodoxy for. All this
for next time, eh?

                          How often we've agreed that there's
no longer a cogent language for gratitude.
Words turn hard in the mouth as if you've literally
bitten your tongue and swollen it. I'm afraid, John,
there is not enough ouzo left to make me chance
those sort of words. Still, I raise what is to all the
overlapping lives our easygoing friendship
comprehends, even in a moonlit stroll round graves.

Renishaw

Sheila Smith

No one has seen
the façade stained pewter, copper,
flickering red, washed with flame
remembering the coal that built it.
Overhung with black, driven trees
("Dreadful weather you had, Mr Piper")
against silver, pierced by weather vanes
and castellations baring uneven teeth.
Yet that is the house.

Behind, in the hanging gardens,
titanic yews are flying buttresses,
exact, sheltering descending lawns
and pools. A fountain with rainbows.
No one has seen
the stone warrior and Amazon ease off their helmets,
relax at the mouth of the Wilderness.
Yet today they look self-conscious
as though just having resumed their poses.
Clipped hedges and carefully disordered trees in place.

The drowned boy in pink velvet,
lounging in his full-length portrait,
no one has seen. Yet quite old ladies
have felt his moist kiss
as they drowsed in the chilly guest-room.

On Midsummer Night
the ancient gramophone's mammoth horn
sets dancing lithe figures in hip-swinging chiffon,
booms poems against syncopated music.
Set in the stable yard
the advanced steam engine
(ordered by the Tsar, but not collected)
once burnt straw powering the saw-mill.
It turns smoothly, burning nothing,
with a little song to itself.

But no one has heard.

Byron at Missolonghi, April 1824

Stan Smith

The midges hereabouts can be ferocious.
Out on the salt pans that girl with doe eyes
Gave me the eye from behind her thingummyjig.
The Albanians are bloodsuckers like the flies
but by God their girls can go. And their bite's atrocious –
the moskies I mean for God's sake! – some are big
as the terns out in the gulf, or Zeus's swan –
and their breasts are like swansdown, out of the sun
that turns their heads brown as the hillsides – one
is speaking of the girls, in Heaven's name!
They turn *my* head. Of afternoons the sun
sits on the water like a sheet of flame.
The cut-throats here will never come to good,
there's fever in the air, and in the blood.

A Stranger, Well Received

Mahendra Solanki

You could not call him one of my own,
his face all mottled pink and red;
even in summer, in tweeds and brogues.

But here, I almost embrace him
as he translates a menu
as foreign as the food:
stewed testicles, stomach of geese,
liver force-fed on maize.

Rhodes: Houses of Bread

Christopher Southgate

A tiny red-tiled church.
Groins of veined stone hold an apse
which frames an altar. A candle
floating in a cup of water
flickers out its flame.

In Ottoman times this place
became the bakery for the Muslim poor.
Its chimney survives as a window.
The walls remember their service —
leaven and ash.

On the beach there is a bakery,
a kind of concrete shack
where a family turns out crusty
caraway-grained loaves, the locals'
daily sustenance.

The place sweats heat
catches the salt-spray
fuses it with woodsmoke, cinnamon,
patience, caraway,
ash and leaven.

Olives

Alicia Stallings

Sometimes a craving comes for salt, not sweet,
For fruits that you can eat
Only if pickled in a vat of tears —
A rich and dark and indehiscent meat
Clinging tightly to the pit on spears

Of toothpicks maybe, drowned beneath a tide
Of vodka and vermouth,
Rocking at the bottom of a wide,
Shallow, long-stemmed glass, and gentrified,
Or rustic, on a plate cracked like a tooth,

A miscellany of the humble hues
Eponymously drab —
Brown greens and purple browns, the blacks and blues
That chart the slow chromatics of a bruise —
Washed down with swigs of barrel wine that stab

The palate with pine-sharpness. They recall
The harvest and its toil,
The nets spread under silver trees that foil
The blue glass of the heavens in the fall —
Daylight packed in treasuries of oil,

Paradigmatic summers that decline
Like singular archaic nouns, the troops
Of hours in retreat. These fruits are mine —
Small bitter drupes
Full of the golden past and cured in brine,

English Destinations

Michael Standen

Fuelled more often than not not by hate
but by the rich disdains most of us have,
we keep on course until we die.
Predestination has more syllables than sense,
and reinvention, though now in good supply,
is hopefully done; but it's questionable
how far we can escape inheritance.
Yet hope can ooze from a dry lack of easy hope
as we bear our freight across a lifetime's sea.
We steer by whatever our starry nativity,
leaking but somehow true and pumpable,
not lost on coastless waters where the cost's
far dearer than knowing where we're bound
to go, but going best we can and as best found.

Listen to the Words

A "fully interactive poetry experience"

Anne Stevenson

"I-pod" is a hideous word,
While "mobile phone", although euphonious,
Chirps from its ambulant nest like a digital bird.
"Blog" is the ugliest word I've ever heard;
As for the razz-ma-tazzda of TESCO and ASDA,
For an epithet that doesn't sound erroneous
Why not try on ACRONYMONIOUS?

What precisely does "interactive" mean?
Just being friendly? Or something more obscene?
Should I "download" the messages I'm "text'd"?
Is making love the same as "having sex"?
The verb "to party" isn't quite the same
As putting your manners on and *going* to one.
No, "partying" is an "innovative" game
Like virtual food, or vandals having fun.

"To be honest" and speak my mind,
Dear John, my guess is that "at this point in time"
English is leaving you and me behind.
Do you know how to teach a sound to bite?
Do I go surfing through a net all night?
Lacking "promotional strategies", I'm afraid
We'll hardly make the canon's hit parade.

Still, appearing "live" at seventy has
A tingling, clear, unsponsored compensation.
Like fugue motifs in Bach, like flowering jazz,
Those plummet lines of language, free of fashion,
Reach to your deepest layer and won't let go.
There, every minute tells you lightly, gently,
The still, sad music of humanity
Is all we know, and all we need to know.

Trees as Artists

Peter Street

We are painters,
natural artists.
Each summer with long arms

using green or sometimes yellow. Just
happy to stand painting your streets,
gardens, roads.

We get fed up
with green, rub it out

But we are soon at it again:
golds, reds, bright yellows!

What to Look for in Winter

Jenny Swann

Homing,
look for traveller's joy or old man's beard,
for stubbled fields

and wintering geese,
for ricks of corn, for grain and chaff
and flowering ragwort,

fieldfare, redwing, thrush,
for withering leaves,
    cow-parsnips smelling of earth,

for rooks
in frosted country graveyards,
yews in berry.

                  Or
orientate yourself for London,
look for the house where you were born,

the out-of-season harvest moon
hanging low, treading ether
over the tower-blocks of Camden.

Look for the skyline
humming now with dusk-twinkle,
pink, grey, mauve, gauzing to purpledom,

look for steam rising from vents,

for figures bowed in on themselves,

for slush-mulched streets,

look for light-flocks,

cluster-berries of shine

bringing you in.

138

Black Moon

Matthew Sweeney

For white he used toothpaste,
for red, blood — but only his own
that he hijacked just enough of each day.

For green he crushed basil in a little
olive oil. His yellow was egg yolk,
his black, coal dust dampened with water.

He tried several routes to blue
before stopping at the intersection
of bilberry juice and pounded bluebells.

His brown was his own, too, applied
last thing in the day before the first
Laphraoig, and the stone jug of ale.

He used no other colours, but his tone
was praised by Prince Haisal, no less,
which got him a rake of commissions

and a residency-offer in Kuwait
which he turned down. At home
the Royal Family was less generous

so he painted them all, in a series
that came to be called his brown period,
though this was strictly incorrect.

He never exhibited with other painters,
never drank with them, spoke of them —
never even spat at their work.

A cave in the Orkneys was his last dwelling
and he rode a horse to his studio.
There were no people in these paintings.

which were found piled up on one another
inside the cave, with no sign of him,
and on top was a depiction of a black moon.

Keeping the Jazzmen Honest

George Szirtes

Keeping the jazzmen honest was no easy task.
You had to prevent them taking the roundabout route
wandering off down byways that don't suit
the gorgeous tunes you give them. And don't ask
which way the wind is blowing
or where they are going.

They think they see beyond music to another music,
a packageful of notes that will just appear.
When not playing by so-called heart they play by ear
their notes grown dense and jungled, damply thick
with ambition and guess
like a drunken caress.

There's something crooked about them. In the late
hours of the night they are plotting the come-uppance
of some harmless little melody not worth tuppence
but innocent as the day is long and twice as straight,
adding barbs, bobs and swings
to my favourite things.

They say it's the heart, but look at their puffy faces.
If hearts they possess at all they're pickled in alcohol
and drowned in the windings of the soul.
Their so-called hearts complicate life, are shady places,
and whether or not you're paying
they *will* keep playing.

Cricketing Memoirs of a 70 Year Old

David Tipton

One thing our father gave us, for which I'm thankful, was a
    love of sport
though this proved a painful enough experience at first;
on the lawn in the back garden I was often in tears —
*"Get to the pitch of the ball..." "Keep that left elbow up and
    your bat straight..."*
It was the constant repetition of a shot until we'd got the
    hang of it.
Competition was fostered — *"Your brother's got the idea, and
    he's younger than you...!"*
But learn we both did and though toys were scarce
we always had a football, boxing gloves and cricket gear.
In August 1945 Dad took us to see a Victory Test Match at
    Edgbaston:
Some of the cricketers we'd read about on cigarette cards
    were playing
— Walter Hammond, Len Hutton, Hassett and the debonair
    Keith Miller.
Later, he bought us junior membership of Warwickshire
    C.C.C.
and at the County Ground, we watched the elegant Hardstaff,
    hard-hitting Grimblet and Martin Donnelly;
then during the long hot summer of 1947 my personal heroes
    — Bill Edrich and Denis Compton
who put on a 100 after tea the year they scored 3000 runs
    a-piece.

"You're not in the slums of Birmingham now, Mr Tipton,
but in St. George's College, the finest school in the Argentine,"
reprimanded the headmaster, a Canon in the Church
    of England,
for arriving unshaven to give my 8am lesson on
    Tudor History
or was it for wearing a green corduroy jacket to Speech Day?
But I vindicated the slums of Birmingham by heading the
    Argentine bowling averages
during the southern summer of 1961-62;
cricket my main claim to fame in the "colony".
One memorable afternoon, the River Plate yellow and
    sluggish, a mile away,
I bowled out six of the Argentine "Test Stars"
with my fast away-swing and late off-cutters
"How do you compare in speed with Trueman?" I was asked.
"Test Stars?" I queried. *"Yes, we play tests against Uruguay*
    and Brazil."
I didn't disillusion them, but went out to bat
scoring fifty with cover-drives, cuts and a couple of satisfying
    hooks
in a partnership with Robinson, the other teacher who played
    as a guest, to win the match for the Old Georgians XI.
Later, they didn't invite us to their party, but gave us —
    professionals — a crate of Cristal beer and a carton of
    Lucky Strike.
That evening the eucalyptus tress were aromatic in the cool
    of twilight
as we supped our beers on the patio in the shade of a lemon
    tree.

Red Label

In Memory of the Martyrs of the Athens Polytechnic 17/11/73

Tim Thorne

Johnnie Walker strides out above Piraeus
like the Byron of our days or some
other arrogantly scotched Pom.
The ferry wake churns the port to mist
as we make for Patmos, where St John
(according to the young bloke in the taverna
— a Nick Giannopoulos fan —) had his "Revolution".
It is easy to relax out of history
and into the past instead, aged and amber,
mellow as the tourist and his drink,
comfortable as the patriarch
smoking at Sunday breakfast in jacket and tie,
worry beads at the ready, just in case.
Harder to be the wog boy out of work
in the diaspora or on the broken streets
under Johnnie's well-shod heel.

There's no need for apocalyptic beasts
roaring like minotaurs out of the precious digs,
scaring the suburban charismatics back home.
John's Babylon whore might just as well
be Delta (or any other of Mark Philippoussis' conquests).

And was it Alpha Tau Omega or Sigma Chi,
the frat house that shaped those CIA boys
who made the '67 coup? Richard Welsh,
Bush senior's buddy, came from "Further west
than your sires' 'Islands of the Blest'."

Now we water our euros till they turn cloudy
and Diogenes flies business class to Brussels,
his lamp a safety hazard, security breach.
So are we all, and worse: unfashionable,
my comrades. Dash down yon glass of scotch and coke.

A Jackeroo in Kensington

John Tranter

With a fistful of dollars in a knapsack
and a brutal turn of phrase, colonials
are crashing the party. *Cette parade sauvage* —
on the skyline you can see Rupert Murdoch
crawling over Fleet Street, a pygmy King Kong —
did they shrug off an empire for this?
Too right, boss, that's what I want to hear,
the glib, slangy lingo of the tango dancers
steaming into Sydney Harbour in a sepia haze —
it's the bottom of the world,
say the blond sophisticates. Hang on;
wasn't "King Kong" invented in America?
*The eyes that look into Australia
are European eyes,* Peter Porter said, but
my friends' kids holidayed in Hollywood,
and live in San Francisco. I'm
middle-aged, and England made me, cobber,
reading Maugham in the shower recess — though
what about Malraux? and Lao Tzu?
I'm going to be a Chinaman
next time around, speaking perfect English —
or Creole — who can choose between
the torrid charms of the one and the
cool, pragmatic bite of the other?
Can you say *You fuckwit!* in Italian?
No way, but if you play Wagner
loud enough you'll get rich quick — rich
in the Bloomsbury sense of the word —
a humus of culture, a knack for sleeping in,
these things adorn you like a froth
and the National Gallery opens its doors
for you, and you alone, at last.

Revolution

Dmitri Tsaloumas

I

Despite the enlistment of
unemployed youths
the rubbishmen can't cope
with the number of heads

children are encouraged
to make neat pyramids of them
in the great city squares
for easier picking

prizes are announced for
numbers and symmetry

the noise is deafening
bands play, shots ring in the air
explosions

bare-breasted women
brandishing angry flags
march in the blood-sunset light
hirsute with bayonets

"down with tyranny" etc.
"make love not war" etc.
et cetera

the festive air's alive
with noble demands

Great officials who managed
to hang on to their heads
sit in the cafés in disguise
over espresso cups

they appraise the mob's
exuberance

masters of vision in the dark
they perceive new possibilities
make plans

the tumbril rolls past
the crowded café windows

the tumbril jerks its passengers

some wigs come off exposing
shiny heads

dogs howl dogs bark
children in motley rags
trail behind banging cans
singing spring songs

hope rises from brimming pots
in every city joint

Carnation buttonholed
the leader stumbles forth to halt
grimly advancing cars of war

unarmed but for a bottle
the great man climbs
onto the stilled hump
of the first creeping-hull

the leader holds up the bottle
the crowd stops breathing

Rejoice fellow citizens
bid fear farewell
markets of plenty will liven up
our lugubrious cities
nights without shadows
will follow sunny days

just then this dove flies in
it carries a twig in its beak

it wheels three times overhead
then dips and lands
upon the great man's head

thereon the dove shits
then flutters off to a burst
of furious joy

the leader climbs down
the charmed monster's hump
leaves it on heaving shoulders

his sainted head beams

hosannas rise more thunderous
than at a Champions League goal.

Carry On at Your Convenience

Deborah Tyler-Bennett

Old man huddled on the Palace Pier, sloped as a displaced
   beach-hut.
Belonging more to the burnt-out West Pier, he hugs a
   Waitrose bag
filled with rat-eased holiday brochures promising Pinewood
   sets
of azure skies and gull-white hulls.
                              He fidgets them, revealing
copies of *Gramophone*. Signs behind him read:
NON-DESIGNER SUNGLASSES/ NON-DESIGNER
                                   PRICES.
Rough laughs break against his head, like cinema crowds
hooting at Charles Hawtrey, Bernard Bresslaw,
Barbara Windsor.

Later, he pads "The Victoria Bar", adrift on splitting
   trainers.
Shifts, clawing the bag, as customers
(dead-spits of Hattie, Kenneth, Joan) holiday round him,
as staff mop spillages.

If this was "Carry-On", the barmaid would lean enormous
   boobs
towards some weedy punter, asking innocently if he
liked the view, barmen sporting names like Widdle,
Endaway, and Bigger endlessly dropping pints.
The old man's magazine? *Wink*
or *Titbits*, not *Gramophone* (unless someone
was to ask did he: "Buy it for the horn section?")

Piped over the bar, Hollywood assaults his ears:
"Move Over Darling"... "Secret Love"...
Doris Day holding notes longer than a Brighton Promette's
    legs
honeyed as the promise of bleached hair.

As he steps out, catch Sid James's randy laugh
undercutting Hollywood's touch of mink.

Hard of Hearing

Hugh Underhill

Somewhere in this morning's early
light a blackbird sings — I think it is — the tune
too distant-tenuous to clearly hear — but yes,
it must be so, a blackbird, for what else?
It comes upon the ear like something
long ago — a time of early
light, unfathomcd voices floating in as if
from oceans round yet to be launched
out into, speech which now's like
shadows in the mind
to be configured fitfully, a reconfiguring
as halting-effortful as those first childmind
figurings — her Sussex speech, yes, *that* stays loud
and clear, today she'd say's her day to go
to Chidester, or maybe for a change straight
off along the coast to Porchmouf. How
recall a voice that came too soon
to ever register as electronic arabesque?
                              Now
this huge wailing sound
comes at us like the tsunami, it is our global
auditory superflux, and all the pain and grief
we hear so near and amplified unlikc
the timelapse-stealth of news
ancestrally.

                              But in the early
light some hard-to-be distinguished
lenient birdsong, reminding me
how some came once, though differently —
much-cited, I'll allow — to Edward Thomas when
all drew to a portentous stop; he who also
wrote of surmised speech
"remote as if in history." Suffice
this blackbird's so faint twiddling now:
it's like the softest kind of love.

A Hundred Swans

Peter Walton

As clean as washing stretched across flat fields
In level winter sun, a hundred swans
Nibble the grass and dip their yellow black-tipped bills
Into black earth for cold fare of the fens.
Two hundred feet are muddied; but the white
Siberian feathers stay unsoiled, remote.

There's nothing else — except a knot of trees,
A crouching house, and miles of straight-drawn
Drainage dykes beginning to unfreeze
In this pressed landscape — we can focus on.
Hypnotic as a pulse of light, these arctic
Bewick's take the scene. Almost domestic

For a season here, yet — wild as water,
Free like moonlight — they're waiting for the stir
Of spring to lift their voices into flight,
And leave an emptier England to the night.

On The Embankment

Huw Watkins

Sunday is the day the city
escapes to the river; the pleasure trips
taking their children on the same dreams
for the price of a week-day's fish and chips.

It is the same river; until you think,
the water has changed and here and there
a new line has been drawn in
or something that once landscaped is no more.

On closer inspection, the swans are too grey
to have been the ones we fed;
the same children feeding them
are all different, a handful of their bread

now costing as much as our old loaf.
And though the reason has not changed,
where we came down in the trolley
and walked to the river, now cars are ranged

along the embankment; ice-cream vans
try for the most insatiable part;
candy floss flows in the river breeze.
On such days the sense of living is caught

like a religion that will not stay indoors
confined by pulpit or pew
or the organisation of it
but moves in its incumbent way

to the sea. There is a thud of ball
on the park only a throw from where
Voce and Larwood are spliced into history,
ghostlier than statues, more real for not being there.

A man fondles his girl along.
A poodle, clipped to its owner's pride,
trots at the end of its compulsive lead.
Parked near the verge, I wait inside

and watching the living think of the dead
in their mustiness; of unknown name,
inessential bone; the thought dark,
fossilizing out of its own time

while she walks
with that promise of love's return
her breasts waiting to break out
like white roses in this dry June.

Elizabeth's Version

John Weston

I could wish, brother, more poetry in him,
less theatre. To scotch Valentines on a whim,
how childish. He thinks I pray at St Olave's
just for the dancing master? Look how I slave
all the year round — I doubt that enters into
his crotchety short-hand. And it's no sin to
lift French minuet above *cazzo dritto*.
I love him, but he risks my love's memento
engrossed with hot tongs where they cut out his stone.
"Prick-louse" must change his tune, or trill to atone!

Stomachful? Yes, I put it all down to fear
the ancient name might founder without an heir.
His bobbin threadless, how could I close the stitch?
So, plagued by his own pest, fired by an itch
to fumble every skirt, he would gad about
like some periwigged Polcinello, played out,
mocked from the quarterdeck. Then pity whispered
"The heart may soon grow sick when hope is deferred:
bolder jointure is easy for your beauty
to conceive — call it a catholic duty."

His fishmonger uncle had already asked
to sire my child for gold (what cod!). But the task
was now to catch seed blown from farther afield,
to spring home-grown. With a birth, I knew he'd yield
and his lion be caged. To Brampton by coach
I fell in with a King's Guard man, whose approach
brought back at once the Lambeth gypsy's riddle
"Fortune's messenger will not ride side-saddle".
We broke the day's passage at The Reindeer Inn.
By candle, many would have been taken in.

A small bird fluttered, and I rejoiced to hide
belly in billowing morning gown. Outside,
Dutch ships sailed up the Thames, and the press of war
kept him as distant as the evening star.
I never told him. But when I lost the child,
feigning simply my months had returned, he smiled
as if some gibbous thought half-formed in his mind,
then turned back to prospects for *The Golden Hand*
and Navy business. As I have since turned back
to painting Our Saviour, and the sun is black.

(Elizabeth de St Michel, wife to Samuel Pepys, died on 10
November 1669 at the age of 29, and was buried in St Olave's
Church, Hart Street)

Hastings Revisited

Merryn Williams

Going back, I found that the buildings were
Gone. Even the old girls'
Grammar school had been wiped off the

Face of the earth. I stood
Faltering. Where could I
Find the landmarks which had shaped my

Early years? All that I remembered
Erased. They seemed to have taken away
Everything.

Down town, I went in search of the
De Luxe cinema. It had been
Devastated.

Cricket is no longer played on
Cool summer days in the town centre.
Coming up Queen's Street, I could hear

Bulldozers. They were boisterously
Breaking the green up, overlooked by
Blank, blind windows. And they've pulled down the

Albert Memorial.

Desperanto

Michael Wilson

Sad poetry. It's written everywhere,
by broken hearts in search of self-expression:
the universal language of despair.

She writes of anguish (and it's hard to bear).
She chisels, from the floes of her depression,
sad poetry. It's written everywhere.

He tries (in vain) to emulate John Clare,
to forge a bridge between his self-obsession and
the universal language of despair.

But he's not self-aware, not debonair,
he lacks the savoir-faire, the self-possession...
Sad poet, try! It's written, everywhere,

that anyone who's sad, and solitaire,
should curse in verse, as if their flair could freshen
the universal language of despair.

And round they go — mad fingers twirling hair
(which tends to give a negative impression:
sad!). Poetry. It's written. Everywhere,
the universal language of despair.

from The Newstead Fandango

Gregory Woods

(NB: The speaker is Lord Byron)

2. The Wandering Rocks

A hot September afternoon, a roasting field of barley,
Largesse in such abundance, all the world seems
    touchy-feely,
And even the most misanthropic farmer waxes jolly.

The Earth is manifest in such variety, it daily
Demands to be acknowledged with an attitude part holy,
Part blasphemous. We owe a duty to esteem it highly

But estimate its future under Man's control but poorly —
Ill-chosen habitat for such a self-destructive bully.
While Satan was condemned to surf the landscape
    on his belly,

Man stands aloof from it, perhaps remarking in its silly
Quiescence his disruptiveness. Could he but fly he'd duly
Remove himself from gravity with levity and sully

The very breeze with his inconsequence... A steeple's hourly
Reminder of mortality rings out across the valley
And fools with time to kill accuse the clock of being early.

3. Nestor

In literature, preserve us from the pleasant and the subtle.
There's not a single English poet whom I wouldn't throttle
In the attempt to shape his feeble voice to something brutal —

Just as I'd rather struggle than relax in matters coital.
It's news to me if life is long enough to waste on little
Particulars. You have to act as if it would be fatal

To sacrifice contingency to comfort. Never settle
For anything predictable. Let every moment startle
With its capriciousness. The man who vegetates in foetal

Suspension looks to me as if he thinks himself immortal.
With every year I add to life's accumulated total
I feel compelled to greater energy, because it's vital

If not to conquer life at least to know you fought the battle.
So, far from slackening, I have in mind, as down I hurtle
Towards oblivion, to press my club-foot to the throttle!

4. Lotos-Eaters

Accumulate a fortune! Live forever! Win the Derby!
Would anything you wished for, drunk, be worth the
    having, sober?
Who but a chump would choose to live as long as Colley
    Cibber

But write as badly? Must there not be more to life
    than jabber
And less than mere longevity? In every living fibre
Of my physique I yearn for not the product but the labour.

If writing verse were like a conversation with one's barber,
And sonnets could be left as structureless as an amoeba,
It might be possible without much thought to shape a flabby

Excuse for prosody. But poetry is not a hobby;
Still less, reliable as compost for the money-grubber.
Deprive me of that will to write and maybe I, just maybe,

I could endure a lifetime nibbling lotoses on Djerba —
Or lettuces, at least. Far rather that than fill my abbey
With supererogatory detritus bought on eBay.

5. Sirens

I'd swear an oath on all the Torahs, Granths, Korans
    and Bibles
A plague of theists can devise, that no affray of Babel's
Was louder than the countryside an English poet troubles.

Wherever oak matures, a pasture slopes and water burbles,
The warbler, faithful to its onomastic fortune, warbles
Among the reeds, and bream play hard to spot above
    green pebbles,

Some twerp, mistaking flatulence for inspiration, dabbles
In poetry, the easy art of self-expression, foibles
Like goitres on display for all to see. He walks, he scribbles —

But knowing nothing of the Nature he applauds he cobbles
Together paperscapes of views he thinks his verse ennobles.
Where once the voiceless woods were resonant with peals
    of bluebells,

His rhyming seems to satirise the silence it enfeebles.
He keeps returning to the slopes on which he lost
    his marbles:
Parnassus is a hill in England, wild with elk and shoebills.

Littlebredy

Kit Wright

At the top of the hill the twisted thorns
Were crouching out of the way of the wind
That raced in over the miles of shivering furze.
The valley air
Was sweet with the honey of yellow-beaked flowers
And across the lake the house
Stared at itself in the olive water.

What had been remembered
By the folk intelligence of the path
That chose that way of all ways through the trees?
Why had the dreaming ice
In the stumbering glacier warmed toward this shape,
Beyond all others,
To hollow out its inclination?

Everything there knew why,
However,
The white-robed cricketers, inexorably,
Had made their way down into the valley
To do their dance of stillness,
To do their courtly dance of almost stillness,
Dancing upon their graves before they died.

A Piece for Two Poets

Lynne Wycherley

(i) She turns from her computer to John Clare

I think you'd pour some "Parish" scorn
on us, living as we do. Self-sealed,
peeling from car to door, 'phone to screen,
hardly seeing what few stars fleck between
hallogens, what first leaves fold,
henna to brown, in this oil-fed heat,
how our children fatten in darkened rooms,
play-stationed, while the lark and you (its
numbers falling) sing the inviolable blue.

(ii) Five glimpses of the Severn (for Ivor Gurney)

Grey-green, mid-tide, it slides at my feet,
too calm to mirror you, sedate
but the sun
        conjures a scarlet hat
and all the fires of Framilode are lit.

            ***

Hock Cliff, the Severn's hook. I face
barbed wire and mud. There's no dysentery
though dark thoughts
                breed here. I trace
wool shreds on the wire, a snared sky.

            ***

How it startles me! Chirrups, chirrs.
'No swank', that ebullient bird
in the reeds,
        a sedge warbler,
echo of you. Outspoken, limber.

Night-walker: you'd take this path between
the bank and moon, bit-work or none,
free, half-fed,
            your thoughts in spate —
the river spreads its thinning light.

Do you remember elver-fishermen
setting their lamps by the shore, red stars?
Now they've gone,
                you move in
supple clauses, slip through our fingers.

Contibutors' Notes

Katerina Anghelaki-Rooke was born in Athens in 1939. She studied foreign languages and literature at the universities of Athens, Nice and Geneva. Since 1963 she has published many volumes of poetry, including *The Body is the Victory and the Defeat of Dreams*, *The Scattered Papers of Penelope, Beings and Things of Their Own* and *From Purple into the Night*. She was awarded the National Prize for Poetry in 1985. Her collected poems were published in 1998. *Translating into Love Life's End* was published by Shoestring in 2004.

Alan Baker was born in Newcastle-upon-Tyne and has lived in Nottingham since 1985. He is managing editor of Leafe Press and runs the webzine Litter. He has three pamphlets of poetry in print, the most recent being *The Strange City* (Secretariat Books).

Michael Bartholomew-Biggs works as a university mathematician and lives in North London where he helps to organise the Poetry in the Crypt reading series. His poetry has appeared in magazines, anthologies and chapbooks; a first full collection is visible on the horizon.

Nick Beddow was born in 1957. He is still here. After banging his head into Nottingham University, he wandered around lost for many years until spotting a gap in the fence. He now leads a Community Development team in Stockport. Still missing Captain Beefheart.

David Belbin is the author of many novels for Young Adults, including *Denial*, and numerous short stories for readers of all ages. He works part time at Nottingham Trent University where he runs the MA in Creative Writing. He and John Lucas edited *Stanley Middleton at Eighty* in 1997.

Peter Bennet lives in Northumberland near the Wild Hills o' Wanney. He has published five pamphlet collections and four books of poetry. *Goblin Lawn: New and Selected Poems* (Flambard, 2005) is a PBS Recommendation.

Paul Binding is a novelist, poet and literary critic, who lives in the Shropshire hills. He spent his early childhood in post-war Germany, the subject of his prize-winning memoir *St Martin's Ride* (1990), and an experience responsible for his internationalism and pacifism. He takes a particular interest in Nordic culture about which he writes frequently for the press, and in animals.

Richard Burns Recent books: in 2006, *Manual, the first 20* (Earl of Seacliff, Paekakariki, New Zealand), *The Blue Butterfly* (Salt, Cambridge) and *In a Time of Drought* (Shoestring, Nottingham); in 2005, *Mávro Fós* (Lalon Ithor, Athens); in 2004, *U vreme suše* (RAD, Belgrade), *For the Living* (Salt) and *Crna svetloba* (Aleph, Ljubljana); in 2003, *Book With No Back Cover* (David Paul, London); and in 2001, *The Manager* (Elliott & Thompson, London).

Nadine Brummer was born in Manchester and now lives in London and Dorset. She has been a lecturer in Social Work at Goldsmiths College, and has had two collections of poetry published by Shoestring Press. *Half Way to Madrid* (2002) was a Poetry Book Society Recommendation, and *Out of the Blue* came out in 2006.

Jim Burns was born in 1936. Poems, reviews, articles in *Ambit, Beat Scene, Jazz Journal, London Magazine* and other publications. His most recent books are *Take it Easy* (Redbeck, 2003) and *Short Statements* (Redbeck, 2006). *Laying Something Down: Poems 1962-2007* will be published by Shoestring in 2007.

Derrick Buttress lives in Nottingham. His poems have been published widely in magazines and broadcast on BBC Radio 4. Two television plays have been broadcast on BBC 2 and several radio plays on BBC Radio 4. He has published three selections of poetry — *Spiking the Boss's Gin* (Mo-saic, 1998), *Waiting for the Invasion* (Shoestring, 2002) and *My Life as A Minor Character* (Shoestring, 2005). A memoir, *Broxtowe Boy*, was published by Shoestring in 2004.

Catherine Byron grew up in Belfast and raised daughters and goats in the West of Scotland. From 2003-6 she held an AHRC Creative Fellowship in Writing at Nottingham Trent University. Her first collection, *Settlements* (Taxus, 1985) was hailed as a "classic of Irish exile". Her most recent collection is *The Getting of Vellum* (Salmon, 2000).

Adrian Caesar was until recently Associate Professor of English at UNSW@ADFA, where he worked for sixteen years, and where he remains an Honorary Visiting Fellow. In 2004, he left academe to write full-time. He is the author of several books of non-fiction and four books of poetry, including his latest publication *High Wire* (Pandanus Press, 2005).

Angus Calder was born of middle-class but honest Scottish parents in Surrey in 1942. He was lucky to watch the great Surrey cricket team of the 1950s and become a decent close-fielder and an adequate second-eleven wicket-keeper. He taught in various universities in Africa and for a long time for the OU in Scotland.

Philip Callow was born in 1924 Birmingham and studied engineering and the teaching of English before becoming a writer. He has published fifteen novels, two collections of short stories, an autobiography, six biographies and eleven collections of poetry. Shoestring has also published a collection of poems called *Pastoral* in addition to *New and Selected Poems*, a novel *Black Rainbow* and his memoir *Passage from Home*. He lives in The Cotswolds.

Gerry Cambridge Books of poetry include *Madame Fi Fi's Farewell* (Luath Press, 2003) and *Aves* (Essence Press, 2007) a collection of prose poems about wild birds. He is the founder-editor of *The Dark Horse*. He is a Royal Literary Fund Writing Fellow in the Schools of Biological Sciences and of Physics at Edinburgh University for 2006-2008.

Peter Carpenter is co-director of Worple Press and an Arts Council Visiting Fellow at the University of Warwick. His fourth collection, *Catch*, was published by Shoestring in 2006; he was a contributor to *London: City of Disappearances* and reviews for *London Magazine* and *Poetry Ireland Review*.

Malcolm Carson was brought up in Lincolnshire and then in Belfast. He was editor of *Poetry Programme* whilst at Nottingham University. He now lives in Carlisle, Cumbria. A selection of his work appeared in the first *Take Five* from Shoestring Press in 2003. His collection, *Breccia*, also from Shoestring, is due out in 2007.

Carole Coates published her first collection *The Goodbye Edition* in 2005 with Shoestring Press. One of the poems from it appears in *The Forward Book of Poetry 2006*. She is published regularly by the literary press and appears in competitions and anthologies. She has also published critical writings.

Mandy Coe Her first collection, *Pinning the Tail on the Donkey* (Spike, 2001) was shortlisted for the Aldeburgh Festival first collection prize. A poem from her second collection, *The Weight of Cows* (Shoestring, 2004) was included in the *Forward Book of Poetry*. She received a Hawthornden Fellowship in 2005.

Barry Cole was born in 1936 in London. Apart from two years' National Service and two years as Northern Arts Literary Fellow, he worked as an editor at the Central Office of Information. He has published four novels and seven collections of poems, including *Inside Outside* (Shoestring, 1998). His poems appear in more than a dozen anthologies, including the Penguin *British Poetry since 1945* and Larkin's *Oxford Book of Twentieth-Century English Verse*.

171

Andy Croft lives in Middlesbrough. His books include *Red Letter Days, Out of the Old Earth, Selected Poems of Randall Swingler, A Weapon in the Struggle, Comrade Heart, Red Sky at Night* (with Adrian Mitchell), *North by North East* (with Cynthia Fuller), *Not Just a Game* (with Sue Dymoke) and seven books of poetry, most recently *Comrade Laughter.* He runs Smokestack Books and writes a regular poetry column in the *Morning Star*.

Simon Curtis was born in Burnley and brought up in Northamptonshire. He taught at the University of Manchester for over twenty years. He has published a chapbook, *Spike Island Spring* (1996) and his third full-length book, *Reading a River* (2005) with Shoestring. He has recently retired to Plymouth.

George Dandoulakis (1950) BA in English, BA in History and Archaeology (Athens), PhD (Loughborough) teaches English at the Hellenic Army Military Academy. He has lectured widely and published essays on Greek and English writers. His translations of Greek poets have appeared in many journals. His translation of *Odes* by Andreas Kalvos and Thurios and *Patriotic Hymn* by Rigas Velestinlis are published by Shoestring.

Barbara Daniels was born in Lancashire and now lives in Wales. Her poetry has been widely published in range of magazines and she has won prizes in many competitions. Six collections have appeared, the most recent being *The Cartographer Sleeps* (Shoestring, 2005), launched at the Ledbury Poetry Festival.

Kathryn Daszkiewicz lives and works in Lincolnshire. She was awarded a writer's bursary by East Midlands Arts in 2001 and a selection of her work appeared in the Shoestring Press anthology of New Writing that same year. In the *Dangerous Cloakroom*, her first full-length collection, was published by Shoestring Press in October 2006.

Tassos Denegris was born in Athens in 1934. He has published six collections of poetry and been translated into English, French, Hungarian, German, Portuguese and Spanish. He has translated many major writers into Greek, including works by Borges, Cortázar, Paz, Dos Passos, Singer and Robert Louis Stevenson.

Alan Dent is a writer and editor of *The Penniless Press*. His latest book is *When the Metro Is Free*, an anthology of contemporary French poetry published by Smokestack Books.

Alan Dixon was born in 1936 in Lancashire. After National service he studied art at Goldsmiths' College and taught in schools in London and Peterborough for 28 years. His first collection of poems, *Snails and Reliquaries*, was published by The Fortune Press in 1964. Subsequent collections include *The Egotistical Decline* (Poet and Printer, 1978) *Transports* (Redbeck, 1996) and *The Ogling of Lady Luck* (Shoestring, 2005).

Sue Dymoke lectures in education at the University of Leicester. Her collection *The New Girls: New and Selected Poems* is published by Shoestring Press. She edited, with Andy Croft, *Not Just a Game*, an anthology of sporting poetry published by Five Leaves (2006).

Robert Etty lives in Lincolnshire. His poems have appeared in a range of publications and his latest collection is *Half a Field's Distance: New and Selected Poems* from Shoestring Press.

Roy Fisher was born and raised in Birmingham. In addition to teaching in schools, colleges and universities, he was for many years a territory pianist in the Midlands and North-west, working with such visiting soloists as Harry Edison, Wild Bill Davison, Bud Freeman, Al Casey and Kenny Davern. His poems are collected in *The Long and the Short of It: Poems 1955-2005* (Bloodaxe, 2005) and other writings are available in *Interviews Through Time* (Shearsman, 2000).

173

Kate Foley is a Londoner by birth who now lives in Amsterdam. For much of her working life she was involved with archaeological science and conservation. Her fourth collection is expected from Shoestring Press in 2008. She is a member of the editorial team of the Amsterdam-based international magazine, *Versal*.

Mike Freeman was born in 1938, grew up on Teesside and went to Sheffield University, with Empson for a tutor. He taught in schools and Manchester Polytechnic, then worked as a publisher's reader at Carcanet Press. He is now a freelance editor, socialist activist in Calderdale, and completing a book on Ralph Fox.

Roger Garfitt performs Poetry & Jazz with the John Williams Septet and jazz composer Nikki Iles. His *Selected Poems* are published by Carcanet and he is completing a memoir, *The Horseman's Word*, for Secker. He runs Poetry Masterclasses for the University of Cambridge Institute of Continuing Education at Madingley Hall.

Manos Georginis is lecturer in English in the Department of Humanities and Social Studies at the Hellenic Army Academy in Athens. Besides translating Cavafy and other Greek poets, he has published articles in various literary magazines. His translation of Dionysios Solomos's *Lambros* is published by Shoestring (2006).

Duncan Glen has been publishing collections of poetry since 1966. His *Collected Poems 1965-2005* was published in 2006 and was short listed for the Saltire Scottish Book of the year 2006. He founded Akros Publications in 1965 and from 1978 to 1987 was Professor of Visual Communication in Trent Polytechnic.

John Gohorry was born in Coventry in 1943. Spent 1960s at University of London, obtaining M.Phil (1970) on Sidney's *Arcadia*. Lived in North Hertfordshire since 1971, teaching Business and Management courses and managing

Teacher Training 2001-2006. Married with nine grandchildren/step-grandchildren.

Andrew Graham-Yooll OBE is the editor of the *Buenos Aires Herald*, in Argentina, and has worked on the *Daily Telegraph* and *The Guardian*. He has over 20 books published, several on the history of the British in South America. He has translated poetry into English, and from English into Spanish.

John Greening His last two collections were published by Shoestring (*The Home Key* and *Omm Sety*). He has recently published studies of Yeats and the poets of the First World War. He is a regular reviewer for the *TLS*. He lives and teaches in Huntingdonshire.

Barbara Hardy is a critic, poet, novelist and teacher, whose many publications include *Severn Bridge, New and Selected Poems* and *The Yellow Carpet : New and Selected Poems* (Shoestring), *Swansea Girl* (Peter Owen and Seren), *London Lovers* and *Shakespeare's Imagination* (Peter Owen), *Thomas Hardy*, *Imagining Imagination* and *George Eliot: a Critic's Biography* (Continuum).

John Hartley Williams has published nine collections of poetry. *Blues* (October 2004) was published by Jonathan Cape. A mysterious prose work called *Mystery in Spiderville* was reissued in paperback by Vintage (2003). In 2007 a new book is forthcoming from Salt: *The Ship*.

Peter Hay is a Tasmanian poet, essayist, activist and ratbag — and Reader in Geography and Environmental Studies, University of Tasmania. He founded, captains, and is sole selector — for life — of the far-famed Thylacinians Cricket Club ("Tasmanians nearing extinction"). Recent writings include *Main Currents in Western Environmental Thought*, *Vandiemonian Essays* and *Silently On The Tide*.

Stuart Henson was an Eric Gregory Award winner in 1979. His first two collections, *The Impossible Jigsaw* and

Ember Music, are still in print from Peterloo. A selection of his work appeared in the *Oxford Poets 2002 Anthology*. His most recent collection is *A Place Apart*, (Shoestring Press, 2004).

Gordon Hodgeon was born in Lancashire in 1941. He has worked in schools, in teacher education and in educational administration. From 1972 to 1996 he was a schools' adviser in Teesside, later Cleveland. He has been active for many years in NATE, and in Northern Arts, Cleveland Arts and New Writing North. These days he helps run Mudfog Press. Collections include *November Photographs*, *A Cold Spell* and *Winter Breaks* (Smokestack, 2006). He lives in Stockton-on-Tees.

Graham Holderness is Professor of English at the University of Hertfordshire, and author or editor of numerous studies in early modern and modern literature and drama. He is also a creative writer whose novel *The Prince of Denmark* was published in 2002, and whose poetry collection *Craeft* (2002) was awarded a Poetry Book Society recommendation.

Warren Hope was born in Philadelphia, Pennsylvania in 1944. He began writing poems in his teens and first published in 1970. He is also the biographer of Norman Cameron, the poet and translator, and the author of several critical studies. He teaches at the University of the Sciences in Philadelphia.

Glyn Hughes Poetry Book Society Recommendation, Guardian Fiction Prize, Welsh Arts Council Poetry Prize, Short-listed Whitbread and James Tait Black. Most recent poetry, *Dancing Out of The Dark Side,* from Shoestring.

Chris Jones was awarded an Eric Gregory Award for his poetry in 1996. His pamphlet collection *Hard on the Knuckle* was published by Smith/Doorstop in 2003. A full-length collection is due out from Shoestring Press in 2007.

Richard Kell was born in Co. Cork. After five early years in India he was educated in Ireland. Latterly he was a senior lecturer at Newcastle Polytechnic and after retirement co-edited *Other Poetry*. His latest publications are *Collected Poems* (Lagan, 2001), *Under the Rainbow* (Lagan, 2003) and *Letters to Enid* (Shoestring, 2004).

Angela Kirby was born in rural Lancashire in 1932. Her poems have appeared in many magazines and anthologies and have won prizes and commendations in several major competitions. She has D.Phil. in Creative Writing from Sussex University and Shoestring Press published her first collection, *Mr Irresistible*, in 2005. She lives in London.

Angela Leighton is Research Fellow at Trinity College Cambridge. In addition to critical books on nineteenth and twentieth-century literature, she has also published poems in many magazines. Her first volume, *A Cold Spell*, was published by Shoestring in 2000, and her second volume, *Sea Level*, is forthcoming in autumn 2007.

Herbert Lomas was born in the Pennines, served with the Indian Army, worked in Greece and at Helsinki and London universities. He translates from Finnish, was a regular critic for *London Magazine* for thirty years and reviews regularly for *Ambit*. His tenth book is *The Vale of Todmorden* (Arc, 2003).

Tom Lowenstein has written both poetry and ethnohistory deriving from field work in northwest Alaska. His last book was *Ancestors and Species: New and Selected Ethnographic Poetry* (Shearsman Books, 2005).

Alexis Lykiard has lived in the West Country since 1970. His published work includes nine novels and many translations from French — Lautréamont, Jarry, Apollinaire, Aragon, Artaud, etc. Most recent books: *Jean Rhys Afterwords* (Shoestring, 2006). The first translation of Benjamin Péret's erotic novel *The Nun* (Creation, 2007), and *Judging by Disappearances — Poems 1996-2006* (bluechrome, 2007).

Clare MacDonald Shaw read English at Oxford and has taught in London, the USA and Nottingham Trent University. A former editor of *Quartz*, her books include *How Ghosts Begin* (Shoestring, 1997) and *Blue Fever* (Blackwater, 1999).

Mairi MacInnes has published, in America and Britain, six collections of poetry, two novels, a memoir, an anthology on censorship, and a dictionary of words about alcohol, as well as numerous essays. She and her husband John McCormick have four children and two grandchildren.

Jamie McKendrick His most recent book of poems is *Ink Stone* (2003). A selected poems, *Sky Nails,* was published by Faber in 2001. He has edited *The Faber Book of Italian Twentieth-Century Poetry*. His translations of Giorgio Bassani's *The Garden of the Finzi-Continis* and Valerio Magrelli's poetry are forthcoming.

Edward Mackinnon works as a translator in Eindhoven in the Netherlands. Shoestring have published two collections of his poetry, *Wising Up, Dressing Down* (2002) and *Killing Time in Arcadia (*2006).

Paul McLoughlin was born in London of Irish parents. He continues to teach part-time in a Comprehensive School and at University, and plays jazz saxophones and flute. Smith/Doorstop published *What Certainty is Like* (1998) and Shoestring Press both *What Moves Moves* (2004) and *Forgetting To Come In* (2007).

André Mangeot lives and works in Cambridge. His two collections to date are *Natural Causes* (Shoestring, 2003) and *Mixer* (Egg Box, 2005). He was runner-up in the 2006 Wigtown/Scottish National poetry competition and is also a member of the performance group, *The Joy of Six*. A book of short stories, *A Little Javanese*, will be published by Salt in 2008.

John Manson was born on a croft on the coast of the Pentland Firth in 1932 and worked mainly as a primary teacher. He has published several pamphlet collections and edited two selections of Hugh MacDiarmid's poems. In recent years he has researched MacDiarmid MSS and correspondence in Edinburgh libraries.

Nancy Mattson moved to London in 1990 from the Canadian prairies. Her first poetry collection, *Maria Breaks Her Silence* (Coteau, 1989), was published in Saskatchewan. Her second, *Writing with Mercury,* was published by Flambard in 2006. She is one of five poets in *Take Five 06* (Shoestring, 2006).

Philip Mead was poetry editor of *Meanjin* magazine for seven years, has edited (with John Tranter) the *Penguin Book of Modern Australian* Poetry (now in its third edition) and is currently teaching Australian literature at the University of Tasmania. He is co-editor of the *Journal of the Association for the Study of Australian Literature* and the author of a critical study of Australian poetry.

Stanley Middleton Born Bulwell, Nottingham. After university and army service became a teacher. Has now published forty-two novels.

John Mole (b.1941) is a poet, critic, and jazz clarinettist with the group "Blue Cockatoo". His poetry has received the Gregory and Cholmondeley Awards, and the Signal Award for poetry for children. *Counting the Chimes: New & Selected Poems, 1975*-2003 is published by Peterloo Poets, and a selection of his work can be heard on The Poetry Archive.

Hubert Moore is currently a writing mentor at the Medical Foundation for Care of Victims of Torture. The latest two of his six full collections have been from Shoestring Press. They are *Touching Down in Utopia* (2002) and *The Hearing Room* (2006).

Blake Morrison was born in Skipton, and studied English at Nottingham University; while an undergraduate played for the same Sunday football team as John Lucas. He has published poetry, literary criticism, fiction, journalism and two memoirs, as well as adapting plays for the Northern Broadsides theatre company. His latest book is a novel, *South of the River* (2007).

Graham Mort is a lecturer in Creative Writing at Lancaster University and project leader for the British Council *Crossing Borders* and *Radiophonics* mentoring schemes for African writers. His latest book of poems, *A Night On The Lash,* was published by Seren in 2004. *Visibility: New & Selected Poems* will be published by Seren in Summer 2007.

Michael Murphy is the author of two collections of poems: *After Attila* (1998) and *Elsewhere* (2004), both published by Shoestring Press. His poetry is included in Selina Guinness (ed) *The New Irish Poets* (Bloodaxe, 2005).

Helena Nelson runs HappenStance Press and edits *Sphinx,* a small magazine focussing on poetry publishing. Her book of poems, *Starlight on Water*, was a Jerwood First Collection prize winner in 2003.

Robert Nye Winner of the Hawthornden Prize, the Gregory Award for poetry and the Guardian fiction prize, Robert Nye was granted a Civil List pension in 2000 for life-long services to literature. His last novel, *The Late Mr Shakespeare*, is currently being adapted for the stage. His latest book is *The Rain and the Glass: 99 Poems, New and Selected*, published by Greenwich Exchange.

Ruth O'Callaghan is one of five poets featured in *Take 5* (Shoestring, 2006). Her poetry has been published in numerous magazines and anthologies and translated into Italian and Romanian. Her first collection is *Where Acid Has Etched* (bluechrome, 2007).

George Parfitt was born in Trinidad but spent most of his working life as Lecturer and then Reader in English Literature at Nottingham University. He has published widely on seventeenth-century poetry and the literature of the First World War. Poems have appeared in periodicals, pamphlets and anthologies. He is married and lives in Newark.

Tom Paulin was born in Leeds in 1949. His latest book is *Crusoe's Secret: the Aesthetics of Dissent*. He is G.M. Young lecturer in English at Hertford College, Oxford.

Heather Peace was born in Sheffield; she studied English at Nottingham University between 1975-78, and has worked as a theatre director and BBC script editor. She has a son and lives in Walthamstow.

Nigel Pickard His first poetry collection was *Making Sense* (Shoestring, 2004). His first novel, *One* (Bookcase, 2005), was called "assured, observant and unsettling" by *The Guardian*.

Chris Pilling Since *The Lobster Can Wait* (Shoestring) he has published *In the Pink* (Matisse poems) and *Tree Time* and, since *These Jaundiced Loves*, a translation of *Les Amours Jaunes* by Corbière, he has translated Max Jacob (with David Kennedy) and Lucien Becker, both short-listed for prizes (the Weidenfeld & Popescu). His *Life Classes* are in *Take Five 04* (Shoestring) and *Alive in Cumbria*, a Lakeland Book of the Year 2006, is of an exhibition of poems with photos by Stuart Holmes, which is still on tour.

Richard Poole taught English Literature to adults for thirty years. He now writes full-time. His publications include five collections of poems and *Richard Hughes,*

Novelist, a critical biography. *The Book of Lowmoor*, a dark fantasy trilogy for teenage and adult readers, comprises *Jewel and Thorn*, *The Brass Key* and *The Iron Angel*.

Peter Porter is an Australian of mixed English and Scottish origins, resident in the UK since 1951. He has worked as a clerk, a bookseller, an advertising writer and a freelance journalist. He has published 17 full collections of poetry, including *Max is Missing*, which won the Forward Prize. Two versions of his *Collected Poems* were published in 1983 and 1999. In 2002 he was awarded the Queen's Medal for Poetry.

Philip Ramp is an American who has been living in Greece for forty years, writing poetry and translating Greek literature into English. Shoestring Press has published many of his translations. He has also published six books of his own poetry. A seventh, *Keen*, is due from Shoestring in 2007.

Arnold Rattenbury was born in China in 1921. After war service he co-edited the radical magazines *Our Time* and *Theatre Today*, later working as an exhibition designer. He published seven volumes of poetry, including *The Frigger Makers* (1994), *Morris Papers* (1996) and *Mr Dick's Kite* (2005) with Shoestring. He lived for over 40 years in the Slate country of North Wales. Arnold Rattenbury died in April 2007 when this volume was in press.

Deryn Rees-Jones's book of essays on 20th century women poets, *Consorting with Angels* ,was published, with the accompanying anthology, *Modern Women Poets*, in 2005. A chapbook, *Falls & Finds*, will be published by Shoestring Press in Spring 2007. She teaches English at the University of Liverpool.

Peter Robinson has published *Ghost Characters* (Shoestring), *There are Avenues* (Brodie), *Selected Poetry and Prose of Vittorio Sereni* (Chicago), *The Greener Meadow: Selected Poems of Luciano Erba* (Princeton), and *Talk about*

Poetry: Conversations on the Art (Shearsman) in 2006. A collection of essays on his work edited by Adam Piette and Katy Price has appeared from Salt. He is a professor at the University of Reading.

Maurice Rutherford was born in Hull in 1922 and spent his working life in the ship-repairing industry. He now lives in nearby Bridlington. His book-length collections, *This Day Dawning* and *Love is a Four-letter World* are both published by Peterloo; the chapbook *After the Parade* is published by Shoestring.

Lawrence Sail has published nine collections of poems, most recently *Eye-Baby* (Bloodaxe Books, 2006). In 2005 Enitharmon published a book of his essays, *Cross-currents*. His anthologies, *First and Always* (Faber, 1988) and, with Kevin Crossley-Holland, *The New Exeter Book of Riddles* (Enitharmon, 1999) and *Light Unlocked* (Enitharmon, 2005). He is a Fellow of the Royal Society of Literature.

Andrew Sant was born in England, has lived in London at various times, but has spent most of his life in Australia. His most recent books are *The Unmapped Page: Selected Poems* (Arc, 2004) and *Tremors: New and Selected Poems* (Black Pepper, 2004).

Matt Simpson lives in Liverpool and has published six collections of poetry, the most recent being *In Deep* (Shoestring Press, 2006). He has also published a book of poems for children, a collection of literary essays, and five commentaries on Shakespeare plays. His work has appeared in many anthologies and in a wide variety of magazines. In 1996 he was poet-in-residence in Tasmania.

Sheila Smith was born in Devon, was a student in London and then moved to Nottingham to lecture at the University of Nottingham. She has written and published poetry since her adolescence; some of her poems have been broadcast on national radio.

Stan Smith holds the Research Chair in Literary Studies at Nottingham Trent University. He has published books on Auden, Edward Thomas, Yeats, the origins of Modernism, and twentieth-century British and Irish poetry. Other poems from his "Journeys to War" sequence will appear in the journal *English* in 2007. The complete sequence, together with a historical-genealogical sequence called "Family Fortunes", will be published by Shoestring Press in 2008.

Mahendra Solanki was born in 1956. His first collection, *Shadows of My Making* was published in 1986. His work has appeared in Britain and abroad, including *The Observer* and *Poetry Review*. He is also author of *What You Leave Behind* and *Exercises in Trust*. He teaches at Nottingham Trent University.

Christopher Southgate has been a research scientist, a house-husband, a bookseller and a mental-health chaplain. A Hawthornden Fellow in 1999, he has published a verse biography of T.S. Eliot, *A Love and its Sounding* (Salzburg, 1997), and two "Shoestringers" — *Beyond the Bitter Wind* (2000) and *Easing the Gravity Field* (2006).

Alicia (A.E.) Stallings is an American poet residing in Athens. She has published two collections of poetry, *Archaic Smile*, and *Hapax*. Her verse translation of Lucretius' *De Rerum Natura* is due out shortly from Penguin Classics.

Michael Standen Born 1937, had a wartime childhood near London. Worked full-time for the WEA, latterly as Northern District Secretary. Five novels, followed by collections of poetry and an opera libretto *Sell-by* for the composer Andy Jackson. Currently managing editor of *Other Poetry* and heavily involved in literary and voluntary work in the North East.

Anne Stevenson is the author of fourteen collections of poetry, a biography of Sylvia Plath (*Bitter Fame,* Penguin, 1990) and a critical study, *Five Looks at Elizabeth Bishop,* published by Bloodaxe Books in 2007. In 2006, Bloodaxe brought out *Poems 1955-2005*, a collection written during a full and much travelled life in America, England, Scotland and Wales. In 2002, Anne Stevenson was the inaugural recipient of the Northern Rock Writers Award. A new collection of poems, *Stone Milk*, will appear in the autumn of 2007.

Peter Street was born in 1948 in Wigan where he still lives. He has published two full collections of poetry, *Out Of The Fire* (Spike Books, 1993), *Still Standing* (Towpath Publications, 1998) and one Chapbook, *Trees Will Be Trees* (Shoestring, 2001).

Jenny Swann has published three collections of poetry. Her first, *Flesh Tones*, was joint winner of the Redbeck Press Poetry Competition in 1999 and her second, *Soft Landings,* was a Manchester City Life book of the year in 2002. Her poems and reviews have appeared in various journals. She lives in Nottingham.

Matthew Sweeney has published a number of books of poetry, most recently *Sanctuary* (2004) and *Selected Poems* (2002), also poetry and fiction for children, and a co-authored chapbook, *Writing Poetry*. He is currently working on a book of short stories. A new poetry collection, *Black Moon*, is forthcoming from Cape in 2007.

George Szirtes is the author of some thirteen books of poetry, the most recent of which, *Reel*, was awarded the T.S. Eliot Prize in 2004. Bloodaxe will publish his *Collected and New Poems* in 2008.

Tim Thorne lives in Launceston, Tasmania, Australia, where he is the Managing Editor of Cornford Press. The author of eleven volumes of poetry, he founded the Tasmanian Poetry Festival in 1985 and was its Director for 17 years. He has worked as a teacher, a glass packer and a newspaper columnist.

David Tipton was born in Birmingham, has lived in Argentina and Peru but has spent the last twenty-five years in Bradford, where he runs Redbeck Press. His most recent publications include the novels *Paradise of Exiles* (1999) and *Medal for Malaya* (2002) both for Shoestring; a travel-memoir *A Sword in the Air* (Appliance Books, 2003) and *Defying the Odds: Selected Poems* (Sow's Ear Press, 2006).

John Tranter has published more than twenty collections of verse. His collection of new and selected poems, *Urban Myths: 210 Poems* (University of Queensland Press, and Salt Publishing, Cambridge UK) won the Victorian Premier's Prize (Victoria, Australia) for 2006. In 1992 he edited (with Philip Mead) the *Penguin Book of Modern Australian Poetry*, which has become the standard text in its field. He has lived at various times in Melbourne, Singapore, Brisbane and London, and now lives in Sydney, where he is a company director. He is the editor of the free Internet magazine *Jacket*.

Dimitri Tsaloumas was born on Leros in 1921. Fleeing the rigours of post-war Fascist Greece, in 1952 he settled in Melbourne, Australia, where he taught in Victorian secondary schools for over twenty years. Has published ten books in Greek and eight in English. His latest book is *Helen of Troy and Other Poems* (University of Queensland Press, 2007).

Deborah Tyler-Bennett is a poet, and short fiction writer. Her first collection was *Clark Gable in Mansfield* (2003) and she also featured in *Take Five*, edited by John Lucas. She is currently working on a second collection.

Hugh Underhill Publications include *The World We Make* (Shoestring, 1996), *Passing Through Glass* (National Poetry Foundation, 1997), *The Actual Hour* (Poetry Monthly Press, 2001), *The Problem of Consciousness in Modern Poetry* (CUP, 1992) and a collection of stories *The War is Over* (Shoestring, 2005). He edits *The Robert Bloomfield Society Newsletter*.

Peter Walton was born in 1936, grew up near Bromsgrove in West Midlands. *Out of Season* (Carcanet, 1977) won a North West Arts award; and his poems have featured in magazines, anthologies and broadcasts and been among prize-winners in BBC's National Poetry Competition. *The Cheerfulness of Sparrows* (Shoestring, 1988) shared John's own ornithological enthusiasm.

Huw Watkins grew up in the Rhondda, South Wales. Publications: *Times* (Poetry Nottingham Press, 1984) and *Reincarnations* (Leafe Press, 2001). His work was included in *Sestet* (Staple, 1995). Started painting seven years ago. Raises money for Farm Africa by showing paintings and reading his own poems about them. Has exhibited regularly at City Gallery, Leicester. In 2005 he exhibited at Mall Galleries, London.

John Weston has lived and worked in China, continental Europe and the United States, retiring as UK Ambassador to the UN in 1998. He began writing poetry in 2002. He was anthologised in *Take Five* (Shoestring Press, 2004). His first collection, *Chasing the Hoopoe*, was published by Peterloo in 2005.

Merryn Williams lives in Oxford and is the editor of *The Interpreter's House*. A widely published poet and critic, she has written about Hardy, 19th and 20th century women novelists and the poetry of the First World War. Two recent novels, *The Chalet Girls Grow Up* and *The Watsons* are sequels to the work of E.M. Brent-Dyer and Jane Austen. She has translated *Selected Poems of F.G. Lorca* for Bloodaxe. Her latest collection is *The First Wife's Tale* (Shoestring, 2006).

Michael Wilson works in Adult Education and Creative Arts Education in the East Midlands. He has written over 80 "easy-reader" books aimed at reluctant readers for educational publishers Hodder Murray. He also writes poetry, songs, drama and fiction; teaches Creative Writing; and performs as a musician and singer, both solo and in an ensemble.

Greg Woods is the author of four poetry collections from Carcanet Press: *We Have the Melon* (1992), *May I Say Nothing* (1998), *The District Commissioner's Dreams* (2002) and *Quidnunc* (2007). His critical books *Articulate Flesh* (1987) and *A History of Gay Literature* (1998) were published by Yale University Press.

Kit Wright is a Kentishman who writes for adults and children and lives in Hackney in North East London. He has often played at the beautiful cricket ground of Littlebredy in Dorset.

Lynne Wycherley is a member of the John Clare Society, and various green groups; she enjoys being a Shoestring poet. She has appeared widely in the poetry press, and was chosen as an "Alternative Generation Poet" (Staple). Her second Shoestring collection *North Flight* (2006) charts a journey to Orkney, Shetland and Iceland.

Acknowledgements

Katerina Anghelaki-Rooke, "Observations of a Mortal" is previously unpublished.

Alan Baker, "Interruptions from the Past" is previously unpublished.

Michael Bartholomew-Biggs, "Someone Had To" is previously unpublished.

Nick Beddow, "A Cautionary Tale" is previously unpublished.

David Belbin, "Postcard from Bruges" is previously unpublished.

Peter Bennet, "Two English Sonnets" is previously unpublished.

Paul Binding, "Guardians" is previously unpublished.

Nadine Brummer, "Perennial" is previously unpublished.

Catherine Byron, "Aqueous/Vitreous: the Humours of the Eye" is previously unpublished.

Jim Burns, "Listen to the Stories" is previously unpublished.

Richard Burns, "*from* Manual" is previously unpublished.

Derrick Buttress, "This is Not the Poem" is previously unpublished.

Adrian Caesar, "Miner's Lamp" is previously unpublished.

Angus Calder, "I.M. Peter May" was first published in *Waking in Waikato* (Diehard, 1977).

Philip Callow, "Piano" is previously unpublished.

Gerry Cambridge, "The Great Things" is previously unpublished.

Peter Carpenter, "Borders" is previously unpublished.

Malcolm Carson, "The Sunday Academicals" is previously unpublished.

Carole Coates, "Water Work" is previously unpublished.

Mandy Coe, "Iridium Club, New York" is previously unpublished.

Barry Cole, "To a Cornet Player, Prematurely Retired" was first published in *Inside Outside: New and Selected Poems* (Shoestring, 1997).

Andy Croft, "Red Ellen" is previously unpublished.

Simon Curtis, "Dorchester Pastoral" is previously unpublished.

George Dandoulakis, "The Ballad of the North Wind" is previously unpublished.

Kathryn Daszkiewicz, "Like Nothing Else in the Habitable Globe" is previously unpublished.

Barbara Daniels, "Dr Johnson" was first published in *The*

189

Cartographer Sleeps (Shoestring, 2005).

Tassos Denegris, "Perama" was first published in *Selected Poems* (Shoestring Press, 2000).

Alan Dent, "Coketown, England" is previously unpublished.

Alan Dixon, "At the Poseidon" was first published in *The Egotistical Decline* (Poet and Printer, 1978).

Sue Dymoke, "Summer Ash, East Lane" is previously unpublished.

Robert Etty, "Somewhere Like England" was first published in *Half a Field's Distance* (Shoestring, 2006).

Roy Fisher, "Little Jazz" is previously unpublished.

Kate Foley, "When the Buddhas of Bamiyan Fell" is previously unpublished.

Mike Freeman, "A Word with Ralph Fox" is previously unpublished.

Roger Garfitt, "Young Lester" is previously unpublished.

Manos Georginis's translation of C.P. Cavafy's "Epitaphion" is previously unpublished; this is the first time the poem has been translated into English.

Duncan Glen, "High Summer 2006" is previously unpublished.

John Gohorry, "Delivering Learning" is previously unpublished.

Andrew Graham-Yooll, "By Way of Invitation" is previously unpublished.

John Greening, "Reading John Clare on New Year's Eve" was first published in *The Rialto*.

Barbara Hardy, "In Praise of John Clare" is previously unpublished.

John Hartley Williams, "Radio Fun" is previously unpublished.

Peter Hay, "Middle and Leg, Alfred, Please..." was first published in *Silently On The Tide* (Walleah Press, Hobart 2005).

Stuart Henson, "Nocturnall" was first published in *Ember Music* (Peterloo, 1994).

Gordon Hodgeon, "Legacy" is previously unpublished.

Graham Holderness, "Bibliotech" was first published in *Textual Shakespeare: Writing and the Word* (University of Hertfordshire Press, 2003).

Warren Hope, "A Private Anniversary" was first published in *Adam's Thoughts in Winter* (Greenwich Exchange, 2002).

Glyn Hughes, "Examples for Creative Writers" was first published in *Ambit*.

Chris Jones, "A Celebration" is previously unpublished.

Richard Kell, "Alaska for Example" is previously unpublished.

Angela Kirby, "Trizonia" is previously unpublished.

Angela Leighton, "Piano Tuner" is previously unpublished.

Herbert Lomas, "Auden at his Villa on Ischia" was first published in *Public Footpath* (Anvil Press, 1981).

Tom Lowenstein, "John Clare in Burleigh Park" was first published in *The Death of Mrs Owl* (Anvil, 1997).

Alexis Lykiard, "Revaluation in the Poets' Pub" is previously unpublished.

Clare MacDonald Shaw, "The Way to Go" is previously unpublished.

Jamie McKendrick, "Autographs" was first published in *Ink Stone* (Faber, 2003).

Mairi MacInnes, "Dancing at Home in the Thirties" is previously unpublished.

Edward Mackinnon, "Ballad of Robert Johnson" was first published in *Killing Time in Arcadia* (Shoestring, 2006).

Paul McLoughlin, "Flugel" was first published in John Lucas (ed) *Paging Doctor Jazz* (Shoestring, 2004).

André Mangeot, "Labour of Love" is previously unpublished.

John Manson, "In Crombie Again" was first published in *East Sutherland and Other Poems* (Reidhmasach, 1985).

Nancy Mattson, "Begin with the Letter 'S'" is previously unpublished.

Philip Mead, "O Lucky Man" is previously unpublished.

Stanley Middleton, "On at the Top End" is previously unpublished.

John Mole, "Fats" was first published in *Critical Survey* and in *Counting the Chimes: New & Selected Poems, 1975-2003* (Peterloo, 2004).

Hubert Moore, "At Readers Bridge" was first published in *Equinox*.

Blake Morrison, "Grange Boy" was first published in *Dark Glasses* (Chatto and Windus, 1984)

Graham Mort, "Jihad" was first published in *New and Selected Poems* (Seren, 2007).

Michael Murphy, "Spring" is previously unpublished.

Helena Nelson, "Shoestring Shuffle" is previously unpublished.

Robert Nye, "Henry James" was previously published in *The Rain and the Glass: 99 Poems, New and Selected* (Greenwich Exchange, 2005) and in *Collected Poems* (Carcanet, 1998).

Ruth O'Callaghan, "Apricots" is previously unpublished.

George Parfitt, "Royal Oak" is previously unpublished.

Tom Paulin, "Sans Souci Park" is previously unpublished.

Heather Peace, "Reading Lawrence in Beeston" is previously unpublished.

Nigel Pickard, "Oval Tests, End of Summer" is previously

unpublished.

Christopher Pilling, "Too Many Ends in View" is previously unpublished.

Richard Poole, "Too Tots of Irish" is previously unpublished.

Peter Porter, "Lines for an English Heine" is previously unpublished.

Philip Ramp, "Greek February and Then…" is previously unpublished.

Arnold Rattenbury, "Three Prentice Pieces" is previously unpublished.

Deryn Rees-Jones, "Two Flowers" is previously unpublished.

Peter Robinson, "On the Mobile" is previously unpublished.

Maurice Rutherford, "Counting the Cards" is previously unpublished.

Lawrence Sail, "Considering Bridget Riley's *Metamorphosis*" is previously unpublished.

Andrew Sant, "The Heathrow to Melbourne Flight" is previously unpublished.

Matt Simpson, "Taking the Hexameter for a Walk" was first published in *Somewhere Down the Line* (Shoestring, 1998).

Sheila Smith, "Renishaw" is previously unpublished.

Stan Smith, "Byron at Missolonghi, April 1824" is previously unpublished.

Mahendra Solanki, "A Stranger, Well Received" is previously unpublished.

Christopher Southgate, "Houses of Bread" was first published in *Easing the Gravity Field: Poems of Science and Love* (Shoestring, 2006).

Alicia Stallings, "Olives" was first published in the *New Criterion*.

Michael Standen, "English Destinations" was first published in *Gifts of Egypt* (Shoestring, 2002).

Anne Stevenson, "Listen to the Words" is previously unpublished.

Peter Street, "Trees as Artists" was first published in *Trees Will Be Trees* (Shoestring, 2001).

Jenny Swann, "What to Look for in Winter" was first published in *New Welsh Review*.

Matthew Sweeney, "Black Moon" was first published in the *London Review of Books*.

George Szirtes, "Keeping the Jazzmen Honest" is previously unpublished.

Tim Thorne, "Red Label" was first published in *Critical Survey*.

David Tipton, "Cricketing Memories of a 70 Year Old" is previously unpublished.

John Tranter, "A Jackeroo in Kensington" was first published in *Southerly* magazine.

Dimitri Tsaloumas, "Revolution" was first published in *Helen of Troy and Other Poems* (University of Queensland Press, 2007).

Deborah Tyler-Bennett, "Carry on at Your Convenience" is previously unpublished.

Hugh Underhill, "Hard of Hearing" is previously unpublished.

Peter Walton, "A Hundred Swans" was first published in Angela Topping (ed) *The Least Thing* (Stride, 1989).

Huw Watkins, "On the Embankment" was first published in *Poet's England 13* (1993).

John Weston, "Elizabeth's Version" was first published in *Chasing the Hoopoe* (Peterloo, 2005).

Merryn Williams, "Hastings Revisited" was first published in *The Sun's Yellow Eye* (National Poetry Foundation, 1997).

Michael Wilson, "Desperanto" is previously unpublished.

Greg Woods, "The Newstead Fandango" was first published in *PN Review*.

Kit Wright, "Littlebredy" is previously unpublished.

Lynne Wycherley, "A Piece for Two Poets" is previously unpublished.

John Lucas

John Lucas is Professor Emeritus at the Universities of Loughborough and Nottingham Trent. He is the author of many scholarly and critical works, including *The Literature of Change*, *The 1930s: A Challenge to Orthodoxy*, *Modern English Poetry: from Hardy to Hughes*, *England and Englishness: Poetry and Nationhood 1700-1900*, *The Radical Twenties*, *Starting to Explain* and studies of Dickens, John Clare, Arnold Bennett, Ivor Gurney and Elizabeth Gaskell. He has published seven books of poetry, from *About Nottingham* (1971) to *Flute Music* (2006). His translation of the poems of *Egils Saga* is an Everyman Modern Classic.

John Lucas has played cornet with many jazz groups in the Nottingham area, where he has lived since 1964 with the artist Pauline Lucas. He runs Shoestring Press.